RURAL ECONOMY OF RAJASTHAN

RURAL ECONOMY
OF
RAJASTHAN

R.L. GODARA

1988

DAYA PUBLISHING HOUSE
DELHI-110006

ISBN 81-7035-038-7

Published by : Anil Mittal for Daya Publishing House
at 1302, Vaid Wada, Nai Sarak, Delhi-110006, Phone : 260116.
Printed at Arihanta Printers, Naveen Shahdra, Delhi-32.
Bound in Bookwrap, Delhi.

PRINTED IN INDIA

Preface

A reliable reflection of our economy chiefly the rural economy, can be seen in the villages as most of the population lives in the rural areas. Village uplift or rural welfare is by and large the overall uplift and welfare of the entire country as the villages form the very backbone of our economy and they are the nerve-centre to control it throughout the country. Keeping this firm conviction in view, it was proposed to undertake the exhaustive and evaluative study of the rural economy of the Sikar district of Rajasthan. This Sikar district is markedly known for its typical topographical and geographical structure—a conglomeration of sand-dunes and rocky spots. It is also well-known for its socio-economic set-up. Looking to its structure, the district has to a large extent its dependence on agricultural sources of income with some leanings on small and large scale industries. The cattle wealth combined with the agricultural base plays a prominent role in forming and furthering its rural economy.

The study titled as "Rural Economy of Rajasthan" has been planned and divided into seven chapters. The first chapter is the introductory one and presents a general view of the Sikar district and the reserarch methodology used in preparing the thesis. The second chapter deals at length with the physical features, area and location, climate and rain fall, population, transport and communication of the Sikar district. In the third chapter land utilization and crop pattern and production, forestry and means of irrigation of the district are described and discussed in detail. The fourth chapter presents a picture of the rural indebtedness and rural finance and investigates the causes of rural indebtedness and various purposes for which they take the loan and suggests ways and means of finding proper avenues of rural finance. The fifth chapter relates to the rural industrialisation and emphasises on the importance of cottage and village industries, their production, management and marketing organisation, and also the major problems that come in their way and their solution. The sixth chapter is on the rural development programme and such other agencies which play a potent part in adding to the advancement of the rural economy and thereby ameliorating the rural conditions. The last chapter draws meaningful conclusions and submits some significant suggestions.

What more remains to say in the Preface and what more need be said beyond expressing my sense of indebtedness and gratefulness to all such persons and institutions as have had contributed as a great deal in various ways to the completion of this research work ? Over the years, many of my friends, preceptors and well-wishers have encouraged me both by precept and by example. It would be in a way difficult to express adequately my indebtedness to them separately. There are, however, a small number of persons whose assistance has been so good and indispensable that they do merit special mention. Among them is Dr. J.K. Tandon, Assistant Professor, Department of Economic Administration and Finance Management, University of Rajasthan, Jaipur, who besides being the original inspirer for undertaking the present project, has all through been a fountain source of unstinted help and encouragement to me. But for his good guidance and scholarly suggestions, the contents of this thesis would not have been possible and so rich. Indeed he made my work a joy. Next, I acknowledge my deep indebtedness to Dr. H.C. Sharma, Associate Professor and Head Department of E.A.F.M., University of Rajasthan, Jaipur for giving me constant inspiration in the pursuit of this project. I acknowledge my special indebtedness to Prof. Om Prakash, Senior Professor, Department of E.A.F.M. University of Rajasthan, Jaipur for giving me valuable assistance very often. I am also indebted to my collegues in the Department of E.A.F.M. and Commerce College, Jaipur for their constant help and enouragement. I also take this opportunity to express my thankfulness to Shri O.P. Gupta for typing the thesis so painstakingly and punctualiously.

R.L. GODARA

Contents

1

Introduction

Rajasthan, the land of Jat and Rajput chivalry, heroism, and romance has always been a firm fascinating object of study for the historian as well as for the poet. The economic welfare of its people, however, has not been able to attract the attention of the economist and the social reformer to the same extent.

Rajasthan, the second largest state of India, was born on the 30th March, 1949 when the late Sardar Vallabh Bhai Patel inaugurated this new State and drew a curtain over a long act in some of the oldest and most glorious of Indian States. The consolidated State, with its area of 130206 sq. miles, represent the whole of what was formerly known as Rajputana minus the former British district of Abu.

The tropic of Cancer just cust the southernmost exterimity of the State. Thus situated, Rajasthan forms the north-western portion of India. The whole of its western and north-western boundary coincides with the Pakistan border, the common frontier with Pakistan being 730 miles in length. Then its northern and north-eastern frontier marches with the Punjab, and Uttar Pardesh until it reaches the Chambal.

1. Physical Features and Natural Resources

As there is no scientific classification of soils in the State. It has been recommended that this should be done in the laboratory of the agriculture department as early as possible. The *Minerals resources* of Rajasthan have vast potentialities. We have recommended intensive survey, prospecting and investigation in case of *Petroleum* (in Jaisalmer, Barmer and Jodhpur district), copper, iron, maganese, tantalite and columbite. In the case of coal we have recommended that it should be made

General Information

TABLE 1.1: Rajasthan at a Glance 1981

	Items	*Year*	*Unit*	*Particulars*
		2	*3*	*4*
1.	Area	1981	Sq. km	342239
2.	Populations	1981	No.	34261862
	(a) Rural	,,	,,	27051354
	(b) Urban	,,	,,	7210508
	(c) Sex Ratio (Male Female)	,,	No. per (000)	919
	(d) Village	1981	No.	37124
	(e) Density	1981	Per sq. km.	100
3.	Net area sown	,,	(000) Hectares	15578
4.	Cooperative societies	1982	No,	18172
5.	Total Electric available for distributions	1981	Milion KWH	4819.75
6.	Roads	,,	Kms	41631
7.	Per capita indicators			
	(a) State Income at constant (1970-71) prices 1981-82	1981-82	Rs	585
	(b) As current prices	,,	Rs	417
8.	Live Stock	1983	000 No.	49486
9.	Production :			
	(a) Food grains	1981	C00 Tonnes	7148
	(b) Oil seeds	,,	,,	644
	(c) Cotton	,,	000 Bales	426
	(d) Sugarcane	,,	000 Tonnes	1413

Source: Basic Statistics Rajasthan 1983, Directorate of Economics & Statistics, Rajasthan Jaipur.

more serviceable, say, by binding it into briquettes. In the case of lead, zinc and silver mines of Zawar, we have suggested that the recommendation of the zinc committee should be followed. Tungsten is an important mineral of this State.

The stones and building materials industry needs considerable assistance by construction of good roads and railway line, provision of labour saving devices, technical guidance, and direct financial assistance.

Gypsum requires detailed investigation and development in the means of transport and communications, particularly in Jaisalmer district. Method of extraction have also to be improved on the lines of Jamsar gypsum mines.

The Mica industry also needs considerable attention. A fact finding committee should be appointed in order to go into the problem of dead-weight rents. There should also be a detailed geological survey of the mica-bearing areas of the State.

In the case of precious stones it has been suggested that the garnet mines of the state should be worked on scientific lines and the emphasis should be on a well developed abrasive industry rather than on ornamental uses of garnet.

Forest covers about 6.07% of the total area of the State. For the development of the forests the suggestion of Planning Commission have been secommended. Proper rehabilitation of the Adiwasi (Bhil) will solve the problem of its cultivation.

In the case of Power Projects it has been recommended that, besides the important project (R.A.P.P.) already under consideration, the Wakal and the Banas rivers should be considered from the point of view of generation of hydro-electricity. The power available in 1951-52 was only eight MW and the total number of localities electrified was merely 42 out of a total of 32241. The per capita consumption was about three units. The supply of potable drinking water in the rural areas had not even been conceived. As regard power position, it is now generating 1713 MW of power and vigorous efforts to further boost up this capacity are being made. More than 19000 villages have been electrified while there were only 42 electrified bastis at the time of the formation of Rajasthan. Over 2.50 lakh wells have been energised. The emphasis on power development could be understood from the fact that over Rs 1000 crores of the state's total plan outlay have been allocated for this purpose alone.

"There is no doubt that electricity will always be a basic element in any formula for progress."

Indira Gandhi

2. Population Pattern

According to 1981 Census total population of the State is 34261862 crores. There has been an increase of 32.97 in the population. The population of Rajasthan has been increasing continuously since the decade 1921-30 and there is every likelyhood that it will grow faster in future. The food production in State is just sufficient to support the present population. As the population problem is an all India-one. It has been recommended that the Government of India should appoint a *Commission on Population* which should consider this knotty problem in all its multifarious aspects. However, it has emphasised that the qualitative aspects of population are as important as the quantitative ones.

The 1981 enumeration operations were conducted throughout the State during the period between February 9th and February 28th 1981. On the night of the 28th February '81 people with no roofs of shelter constituting the houseless population were enumerated.

Our rural population constituting about 79 per cent of the aggregate population resides in 34968 villages. The Census operations have revealed that there has been a decline in the number of population villages in six districts, viz. Jhunjhunu Ajmer, Pali, Bhartpur, Bundi and Kota between 1971-81 while others have returned a rising trend. Similar variations which were observed during previous Census also may be include some reasons.

(a) Consequent upon extensions in the municipal limits the neighbouring villages were fully merged in the town by Government notification and were therefore, deleted from the village list.

(b) Plans treated as villages in 1971 Census were declared towns before 1981 thus calling for their omission from the village list.

(c) In a few cases small villages were merged with their largest sized neigbours.

(d) Some villages were transferred to other districts because of inter district transfers under Government notification.

The trend in rural population is an equally interesting study. The rural population figures clearly indicate that the rate of growth is not as high as that of urban population. Even so, in the past eighty years the rural folks have multiplied more than three times from 1901 base of 87 lakhs to 270 lakhs. While nearly 43 lakhs persons were added in the rural population during the first fifty years (1901-51) the net increase in the last thirty years has been to the extent of 140 lakhs. In the past ten years alone about 58 lakhs new arrival joined the rural population, outnumbering the figures added during the first fifty years of the present century. The trend is noticeable in all Censuses except that of 1921 both at the State and district level.

The sex ratio of state which works out to 919 according to 1981 Census has confined to be advanced to women. However, varying as it does from place to place, it ranges from 811 in Jaisalmer to 1045 in Dungarpur. Rural and urban areas have revealed sex ratio as 930 and 877 respectively. However,

TABLE 1.2: **Distribution of Rural Population of Workers by Sex, Rajasthan, 1981**

(*000 No.*)

Classification	*Male*	*Female*	*Total*
1	*2*	*3*	*4*
1. Main workers	7149	1380	8529
(a) Cultivators	5242	995	6237
(b) Agricultural labourers	484	229	713
(c) Household industries Manufacturing, Processing, Servicing and Repairs	206	28	234
(d) Other workers	1217	128	1245
2. Marginal workers	163	1878	2041
3. Non workers	6702	9780	16482

Source: Basic Statistics, Rajasthan, 1983, Directorate of Economics & Statistics, Rajasthan, Jaipur.

significantly sex ratio is high in villages as compared to towns and varies from 822 in Jaisalmer district to 1056 in Dungarpur district.

Within the State, twelve districts have bigger share of rural population that is higher than the State avarage the most notable being Banswara district (93.78·/.) followed by Dungarpur (93.54%), Jalor (91.94%), Barmer (91.22%) and Alwar (88.92%) districts

3. Agricultural Improvement

Rajasthan is mainly a foodgrains producing tract. The area under different crops has increased since 1950-51. But there is no reason to be unduly optimistic. Agriculture still depends, to a very large extent, upon the mercy of fickle rainfall. Moreover, the production figures are only estimates. Crop-cutting experiments are still at an experimental stage. We recommended that these should be extended over all the crops. It has also been recommended that survey and settlement operations over the remaining parts of the State should be completed as early as possible. We have also recommended that the statistical section of the land records and agriculture department should work in cooperation and the publication dealing with agricultural statistics should be published annually and regularly.

The problem of sub-division and fragmentation of agricultural holdings is an accute in Rajasthan. We have recommended compulsory consolidation of scattered holdings, particularly in the Jaipur, Kota, and Udaipur divisions. Regarding 'Family holding' we have accepted the definition (the income approach) as given in the draft of the Seventh Plan.

We have emphasised that there should be provisions for regulating the standard of cultivation and management of land. To meet the problem of soil erosion we have suggested that the recommendation of the Planning Commission in this regard should be followed.

Of the total area sown, only about 15 per cent is irrigated. Water is worth the value of gold in Rajasthan. Although some progress has been made during five year plans. We have recommended that an expert committee should be appointed in order to investigate the possibilities of irrigation in the desert as well as the non-desert areas.

The techniques, equipment and organisation of agriculture require improvement. In regard to implements we have recommended that the State Government should set a regular workshop in order to manufacture improved implements, as has been done by the Government of Uttar Pardesh. In order to find out the effect of mechanised farming, particularly tractor cultivation on our soil we have recommended that there should be a careful study of individual regions and soils.

In the case of use of chemical fertilizer we have recommended that experiment should be conducted on different types of soils before the use of such fertilizers is recommended to our farmers.

For the multiplication and exprimentation of improved seeds we have recommended that the government experimental farms should be thoroughly equiped and rationalised.

The live-stock of the State require more attention. We have recommended that the professionaly, nomadic breeders, the Rebaris and Charans, should be settled on land and their methods be brought in line with scientific cattle breeding. We have also recommended that the Gaushala and Pinjrapoles should be turned into cattle-breeding-cum-dairy units. The number of cattle-breeding farm should be increased. There is also a need to improve the breeds of camels and goats which have deteriorated during recent years. We have recommended that the farmers should be taught and encouraged to prepare ensilage of fodder. The possibilities of farming fodder cooperative societies should be investigated. We have also recommended that the Government should preserve fodder in times of plenty in order to sell it to the formers in the times of famines and scarcities. The veterinary hospitals and dispensaries have to be equiped adequately.

In the case of agricultural marketing and finance we have suggested that the recommendation of the All India Rural Credit Survey Committee should be followed.

The agrarian problems of the State have attracted considerable attention and a number of legislations have been passed since integration. We have recommended that the Tenancy Act should be put into force as early as possible.

In regard to the possibility of increase in land revenue we have recommended that looking to the history of land revenue in Rajasthan there is a possibility of increasing it only in accordance with the recommendations of the Taxation Enquiry Commission.

TABLE 1.3: Agriculture and Live-Stock Land Utilisation Rajasthan, 1981-82

	Classtfication	*000 Hectares**	*Percentage to Total Hectares*
1.	Geographical Area		
	(For the land utilisation purposes)	84234	100%
	(a) Forest	2077	6.07
	(b) Land put to non agricultural uses	1512	4.42
	(c) Barren and unculturable land	2960	8.65
	(d) Permanent pastures and other grazing land	1836	5.30
	(e) Land under misc.	32	.09
	(f) Culturable waste	6207	18.13
	(g) Current fallow land	1969	5.75
	(h) Other fallow land	2063	6.03
	(i) Net area sown	15578	45.50
2.	Area sown more than once	3019	19.38
3.	Total cropped area	18597	54.32

*Percentage to net area sown.

Source: Basic Statistics, Rajasthan, Directorate of Economics & Statistics, Rajasthan, Jaipur.

TABLE 1.4: **Production of Principal Crops, Rajasthan**

(000 Tonnes)

Crops	1980-81	1981-82
1. Cereals	5327	5629
2. Pulses	1170	1519
3. Oil seeds	382	644
4. Sugarcane	1164	1413

Source: Basic Statistics Rajasthan, Directorate of Economics & Statistics, Rajasthan, Jaipur.

The agriculturist, who was never certain of the fruits of his labour, abandoned his fields, and at length his country. Mechanised industry could not compensate, and left them at the mercy of unlicensed money lenders. In a very few years Mewar lost half of her population, her lands lay waste, her mines were unworked, and her loome, which formerly supplied all round, forsaken; the prince partook of the general peniry; instead of protecting, he required protection.

4. Rural Industrialisation

Among industries, cottage and small scale industries predominate. But most of these are fighting a losing battle against modern large-scale industries. The case of the revival of these industries is strong. However, a policy of discriminative protection for cottage and small scale industries has been recommended. Those industries which have little or no hope for revival and survival, e.g. hand spinning, manufacture of swords, daggers, bows and arrows, manufacture of kuppis, etc. should not be encouraged or protected. In the case of large scale industries we have suggested that there is still scope for the establishment of a cotton textile unit, a sugar factory in Kota division and a cement factory at Chitorgarh. We have also proposed that the State Government should look into the problem of availability of raw materials and power and other concessions.

We have also recommended that all the loans to varions industries should be given through the Corporation alone.

In the matter of trade unions and industrial relations the neccessity of human relation has been emphasised.

Industrial development is also taking place in the State quite speedily. Now the infrastructure for setting up industries is also complete in Rajasthan. In all potential areas, industrial estates have been developed. There are 171 industrial areas at present in the State when facilities of road, power, water, bank, post office, dispensary, transport, etc. are available.

Khadi and village industries become an integral part of our economic plans. Rural industrialisation provides clinical remedies to many socio-economic ills. Village industries have a capacity to create more employment-opportunities with low investment and shorter gestation period. These industries are generally labour-intensive. The capital required per person employed is much smaller than in the case of large scale industry. Thus, they are ideal for rural areas where capital is scarce while labour is abundant. The features of rural industries and its role in the rural economy is highly important also.

TABLE 1.5: **Central and State Aid to Village Industries Rajasthan**

(000 Rs)

Industry	*1980-1981*		*1981-1982*	
	Loan	*Subsidy*	*Loan*	*Subsidy*
1. Bee keeping	—	—	—	—
2. Edible oils	—	—	940	56
3. Gur and khandsari	—	—	47	16
4. Hand made paper	—	—	—	—
5. Hand pounding of rice	—	—	428	126
6. Leather	—	286	8558	1186
7. Non edible oil soap	—	—	160	15
8. Pottery	—	—	1312	614
Total	—	286	11745	2013

Source: Basic Statistics Rajasthan, 1983, Directorate of Economics & Statistics, Rajasthan, Jaipur.

While going through the Table it is very much clear that leather industry got highest priority in villages industry.

TABLE 1.6: **Village Industry Rajasthan**

(*Lakhs Rs*)

Industry	Production Value		Sale Value	
	1980	*1981*	*1980*	*1981*
1. Ghani oil	794.95	1134.97	901.85	1240.48
2. Gur and khandsari	414.69	284.95	484.87	346.92
3. Hand made paper	43.84	42.71	46.96	44.90
4. Non edible oil soap	104.22	66.48	107.48	68.28
5. Leather	567.27	894.64	799.29	1049.55
6. Pottery	161.30	170.27	177.31	221.95
7. Bee-keeping (Honey)	.47	.17	.41	.25
8. Hand pounding of rice	68.67	61.04	61.76	68.65
Total	2155.41	2655.23	2579.93	3040.93

Source: Basic Statistics Rajasthan 1983, Directorate of Economics & Statistics, Rajasthan, Jaipur.

5. Rural Finance

The co-operative movement is still in infancy in the State. For the rehabilitation and development of movement the recommendations of the All-India Rural Credit Survey Committee have been largely, though not solely, suggested. Instead of the present small primary credit societies, bigger societies with limited liability and covering larger areas has been recommended.

The financial position of most central banks is very deplorable. The only resolution lies in the major state partnership (through the apex bank) in the share capital of central banks. Loans to merchant and traders should be discouraged and finally eliminated altogether. The cooperative long term credit movement is extremely weak. The non-credit cooperation is still very undeveloped. In the case of cooperative marketing the suggestions put forward by the All India Rural Credit Survey have been recommended. Cooperative housing has succeeded in urban areas. Efforts should be made to start such societies in rural areas as well, particularly in the larger village.

The banking system in Rajasthan is composed of two parts, indigenous and modern. The experience in other part of India shows that to modernise the indigenous bankers and money lenders is not easy. Our attitude towards the money lenders and indigenous bankers should neither be of hostility nor of hatred and indifference. In the case of those petty money lenders who just earn a moderate income, attempt should be made to associate them with the vast co-operative banking and non banking structure.

The development of a modern banking is a recent phenomenon. The State associate scheduled banks of Rajasthan, namely the Bank of Bikaner and the Bank of Jaipur, will be merged with the State Bank of India.

It is clear that loans distributed by co-operative and commercial banks have been increased year after year due to expension of branches at block level. The annual capacity of loan distributed by commercial banks are more than that distributed by co-operative banks. Refinance from NABARD and IDBI have been calculated on the basis of on going schemes.

TABLE 1.7 **Ratio of Credit Deposit**
(as on June, 1982)

Group	*Public*	*Private*	*Total**
1	*2*	*3*	*4*
1. Rural	77.0	79.6	87.1
2. Semi-urban	59.4	62.3	60.2
3. Urban/Metropolitan	73.6	54.2	71.0
4. Total	69.7	60.2	70.7

**Including Regional Rural Banks.*

Source: Basic Statistics Rajasthan, 1983 Directorate of Economics & Statistics, Rajasthan, Jaipur.

6. Rural Development Programmes

The 20-Point Programme is an agenda for national action to promote social justice and economic growth. A system of monthly progress reports has already been established by the Planning Commission, which provides a quick assessment of this programme.

The war on poverty is our first priority. In the past five years, more than ten crores of our poor have been raised above the poverty line. Our goal is to remove poverty and create fuller employment.

The 20-Point Programme is the cutting edge of the plan for the poor. The programme has been restructured in the light of our achievements and experience and the objectives of the Seventh Plan. The restructured programme renews our commitment to :—

—Eradicating poverty
—Raising productivity
—Reducing income inequalities
—Removing social and economic disparities, and improving the quality. Twenty points are as follows:

1. Attack on rural poverty
2. Starategy for rain fed agriculture
3. Better use of irrigation water
4. Bigger harvest
5. Enforcement of land reforms
6. Social programmes for rural labour
7. Clean drinking water
8. Health for all
9. Two child norm
10. Expansion of education
11. Justice to Scheduled Castes and Scheduled Tribes
12. Equality for women
13. New opportunities for youth
14. Housing for the people
15. Improvement of slums
16. New strategy for forestry
17. Protection of the environment
18. Concern for the consumer

19. Energy for the villages
20. A responsive administration

Impact of These Programmes

Regarding 20-Point Programme, Rajasthan have shown an excellent performance by achieving more than 90% of annual targets fixed for 1982-83 to 1984-85 in the implementation of the 20-Point Programme. The Rajasthan Cooperative Housing Finance Society has assured a loan of Rs 12500 to each of the *Kacni Basti* dweller who is holding a Patta. Now, Rajasthan has been adjudged the second best State in the country in the implementation of the 20-Point Programme during 1986-87. However, the State surpassed the target set under the IRDP, NREP, Rural Landless Employment Guarantee Programme and the Surplus Land Programme.

—On the food front Rajasthan has been able to make a major break-through. The annual agricultural production that was a meagre as 29 lakh tonnes in 1951 has already crossed the mark of over one crore tonne in 1985-86 as the result of increase in irrigation potential, greater use of fertiliser and soil improvement programme.

—While three decades ago the State was generating just 8 MW of power, it was now generating over 1800 MW of power and vigorous efforts to further boost up this capacity are being made.

—More than 21000 villages and towns have been electrified while there were 42 localities electrified at the time of formation of Rajasthan.

—Similarly, drinking water has been made available in over 24000 villages out of 34000 villages. Concrete steps have been taken to solve the drinking water problem during the last two years.

—Along with these steps industrial development is also taking place in the State quite speedily. Now the infrastructure for setting up industries is almost complete in Rajasthan.

—As every body is aware of the great Thar desert spread over in area of 2 lakh sq. kms. in eleven districts of the State. For restoration of the ecological balance and economic development Desert Development Programme (DDP) was started in 1977-78.

—Under the (IRDP) Integrated Rural Development Programme 91895 families have been benefited during the year 1986-87.

—It is known that Rajasthan is affected by drought. Thus against the target of creating 3,90,000 Mandays, 1134000 Mandays have been created from April 1985 to February 1986 in the State.

—In the field of National Rural Employment Programme Rajasthan has achieved 291 per cent targets.

– 105 per cent in bonded labour,

—107 per cent in electrification,

—135 per cent in slum improvement, and

—154 per cent targets have been achieved in Rural Landless Employment Guarantee Programme.

—The poor by bringing them above the poverty line the performance of the Rajasthan Government has been charitable. In Scheduled Caste welfare 99,790 and 52161 Scheduled Tribe have been benefited

—Against a target of planting 820 lakh sapling, 859 lakh saplings have been planted. To help develope alternative source of energy 3884 bio-gas plants have been constructed

—In respect of the district-wise implementation of the programme Jhunjhunu secured first position followed by Udaipur, Ajmer, Alwar, Banswara, Bhilwara. Bhartpur and Jodhpur, also made noteworthy contribution in enabling the State to secure second position in the country.

In a nut-shell, what needs to be underlined is the fact that of all the development programmes in Rajasthan, the focal point has been the common man and the ultimate index of the success is the people's appreciation of these efforts. It will motivate the administrative machinery to work harder towards promoting a healthier and happier society.

—The achievement under the rural and small industries sector is also very impressive. About 20000 families have been benefited under this point.

—A sum of Rs 12 crore for implementation of various schemes under the Boarder Area Development Programe (BADP) in Rajasthan during the current financial year. Thirty school buildings, 10 primary health centres, 50 community centres and 18 new roads will be constructed under the programme. "The Planning Commission had rated the performance of the State as "very good" in nine points and 'good' in another points of the programme for exceeding the targets during the period."

Findings

—The achievement was more than hundred per cent in case of all the points. It was about eleven times of the target in case of National Rural Employment Programme and more than two times in case of allotment of house sites to poor.

—The progress in other sector in development like education, medical and health, drinking water, desert development and tribal area development has been equally commendable. Rajasthan is, thus, making untiring efforts to ensure a better and fuller life for its people. The achievements of the State assume significance in view of the recuring famines which the Planning Commission had rated as "very good" in nine points.

TABLE 1.8: **Rajasthan—Twenty Point-Programme (Progress Statement) Year 1985-86**

S. No.	*Programmes*	*Unit*	*Target 1986*	*Achievement 1986*	*Achieved Percentage*	*Degree*	*Annual Target*
			April to February	*April to February*			
1	*2*	*3*	*4*	*5*	*6*	*7*	*8*
1.	Integrated Rural Development Programme (I.R.D.P.)	No	73,289	91895	237.68	A	83000
2.	National Rural Employment Programme (N.R.E.P.)	Lakh Mandays	39.02	113.41	290.64	A	45.00
3.	Rural Landless Employment Guarantee Programme	Lakh Mandays	37.28	49.34	133.96	A	43.00
4.	Allocation of surplus land	Hectare	8770	7906.10	90.15	A	10000
5.	Bonded labour	No.	884	926	104.75	A	1032
6.	Help to Scheduled Caste	No.	108840	92790	91.68	A	120000
7.	Help to Scheduled Tribe	No.	54601	52161	95.53	A	60200
8.	Drinking water	No.	1403	1228	91.38	A	1600

(Contd.)

1	2	3	4	5	6	7	8
9.	(A) Housing facilities (plot allocation)	No.	27210	60421	222.05	A	30000
	(B) Housing facilities	No.	27210	26161	96.14	A	30000
10.	(A) Improvement of slums	No.	49885	67484	135.20	A	55000
	(B) House for weaker section	No.	9537	8679	91.00	A	11000
11.	(A) Electrification of villages	No.	837	893	106.69	A	1000
	(B) Energy for villages through (pump set)	No.	8570	8683	101.32	A	10,000
12.	(A) Forestry Development	No.	792.94	858.61	108.20	A	820
	(B) Bio-gas	No.	4135	3884	93.93	A	5000
13.	Two child norms	No.	251655	229339	91.13	A	285000
14.	Health for all	No.	8	40	500.00		10
15.	Fair Price Shops	No.	—	174	116.00		150
16.	Small Industries Development	No.	—	4871	97.42		5000

Source: Directorate of Information and Public Relations, Rajasthan, Jaipur.

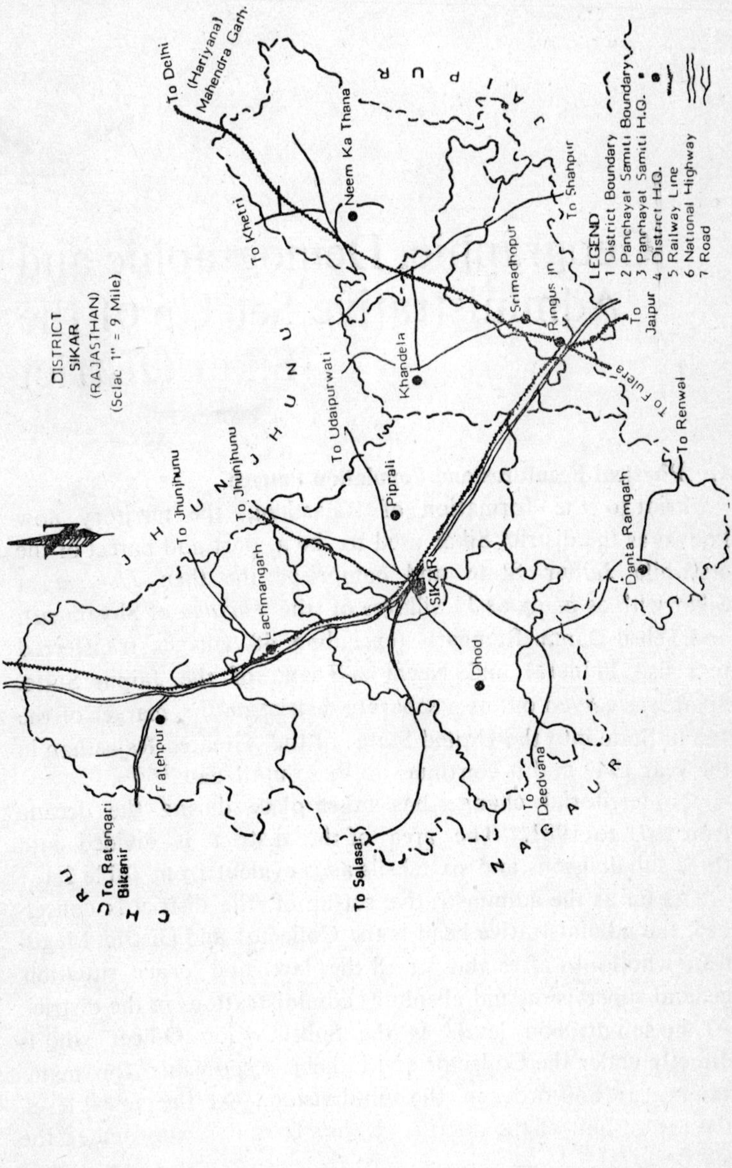
DISTRICT
SIKAR
(RAJASTHAN)
(Sclae 1" = 9 Mile)
To Delhi
(Hariyana)
Mahendra Garh.
To Khetri
Neem Ka Thana
Srimadhopur
To Shahpur
Ringus Jn
To Jaipur
To Fulera
Khandela
To Udaipurwati
To Jhunjhunu
To Jhunjhunu
J H U N J H U N U
Piprali
Lachmangarh
SIKAR
Fatehpur
To Ratangarh Bikanir
C H U R U
To Salasar
Dhod
To Deedvana
N A G A U R
Danta Ramgarh
To Renwal
LEGEND
1 District Boundary
2 Panchayat Samiti Boundary
3 Panchayat Samiti H.Q.
4 District H.Q.
5 Railway Line
6 National Highway
7 Road

2

Geographic, Demographic and Administrative Set-Up of the Sikar District

1. Physical Feautures and Population Pattern

Prior to the formation of Rajasthan, the territory now known as the district Sikar used to be a part and parcel of the erstwhile Jaipur State and comprised the then *Thikana* of Sikar with as many as 11 villages of the *Thikana* of Shyamgarh and Tehsil Danta Ramgarh (excluding 48 villages transferred to Tehsil Phulera) and Neem-ka-Thana of the Jaipur State. Sikar was carved out as a separate district on the marger of the Jaipur State into the United State of the Greater Rajasthan in the year 1949 and it continues to be so uptil date.[1,2,3]

No territorial change has taken place during the decade fron 1971 to 1981. The area of the district is divided into three sub-divisions and six tehsils as is evident from Table 2.1.

As far as the administrative set-up of the district is concerned, the administrative head is the Collector and District Megistrate who looks after and for all the law and order situation, general supervision and absolute administration in the district. At the sub-division level, is the Sub-Division Officer who is directly under the Collector and is held responsible for maintaining law and order in the sub-division. At the tehsil level, the lowest unit of the district, is the Tehsildar who under the

1. Col. I.C. Brooke, *Political History of the State of Jaypore*, (Calcutta 1968), p. 8.
2. Dr. M.L. Sharma, *History of Jaipur State* (1969), pp. 22, 25.
3. Tod James, *Annals and Antiquities of Rajasthan*, Vol. III, ed. W. Crook (1920), p. 1378.

TABLE 2.1: **Administrative Set-up of the District**

S. No.	*Name of Sub-Division*	*Name of Tehsil*
1.	Fatehpur	(a) Fatehpur (b) Lachhamangarh
2.	Sikar	(a) Sikar (b) Danta Ramgarh
3.	Neem-ka-Thana	(a) Neem-ka-Thana (b) Srimadhopur

Source: Rajasthan District Gazetteers, Sikar, Year 1978, Gazetteer of India.

control of the S.D.O. maintains law and order and administers the revenue duties. Panchayat Samities also work at this level.

With the advent of decentralisation in 1959, eight Panchayat Samities were formed in this district. The Panchayat Samities function under the control of a Pila Parishad headed by Zila Pramukh as its chairman but they are administratively supervised by the Collector of the district, who is also an ex-officio district development officer. The Panchayat Samities constitute the main agency of all developmental activities for the rural area. Table 2.2 brings out the position regarding jurisdiction of Panchayat Samities, vis-a'-vis tehsils.

(*i*) *Area and Location*

The district of Sikar is popularly known as the 'Gateway of Desert'. Sikar district is situated on the north-eastern part of the Rajasthan State. Administratively the district is divided into six tehsils and for development purpose into eight Panchayat Samities. The district is characterised by frequent drought and famine conditions.

The district lies between 27°21′ and 28°42′ north latitude and 74°44′ and 75°25′ east longitude at an average height of 432.21 M. above the mean sea level. It is bound on the north-west by Churu district, on the south-west by Nagaur and on the south-east by Jaipur district. It also touches Mahendragarh district of Haryana on its north-east corner. Sikar district is spread over 7732sq. kms. in area running from south to north. The district is divisible into two main topographical areas. The western region is characterised by sand dunes. There is perennial river. But there are five streams in the western region, namely, Mandha, Kantli, Doha, Krishnawati and Sabi. The Aravalli hills divide the district into two parts. The sandy tract single cropped area is composed of Fatehpur, Lachhmangarh and Sikar tehsils, while comparatively fertile double cropped area consists of Danta Ramgarh, Neem-ka-Thana and Srimadhopur tehsils.

TABLE 2.2: **Jurisdiction of Panchayat Samities vis-a'-vis Tehsils During the Year 1983-84**

S. No.	*Name of Tehsils*	*S. No.*	*Name af Panchayat Samities*
1.	Fatehpur	1.	Fatehpur
2.	Lachhmangarh	2.	Lachhmangarh
3.	Neem-ka-Thana	3.	Neem-ka-Thana
4.	Srimadhopur	4.	Khandela
5.	Danta Ramgarh	5.	Srimadhopur
6.	Sikar	6.	Danta Ramgarh
		7.	Piprali
		8.	Dhond

Source: Rajasthan District Gazetteers—Sikar, Year 1978, Gazetteer of India.

(*ii*) *Minerals*

The district occupies a prominent place in production of the minerals specially non-metallic minerals, among the metallic minerals, copper is the most important mineral which has been found out at Dariba, Neem-ka-Thana. It is also found at Maleshwar, Ahirwala and Muthooka, Bihar, Khoni and Salwari. Iron deposits are located at Raipur, Bagoti-Sirohi and Pachlongi-Sirohi. Among the non-metallic minerals apatitue, calcite, dolomite, flourite, lime stone and private pyrnihatite, mica and talc are important. Besides these, barytes, mica, quartz and silica are also extracted. The occurrence of melybalnite and radioactive minerals in Khandela-Ghateshwar area are still under investigation. In addition, stones used for building purposes are found all over the district.

(iii) Soil

The soil survey works were started in Sikar district during the year 1977-78 under the Desert Development Programme. Two types of soil survey, viz. detailed soil survey and reconnaissance soil survey are being conducted by the soil survey unit. There is also one mobile soil testing van functioning in the area. The detailed soil survey is normally carried out in the areas affected by soil erosion and having good agricultural potential. It recommends about better soil and water management for watershed planning and intensive agricultural purposes. Detailed surveys were completed in 24 lakh hectares during the period from 1978-79 to 1982-83 which include the village area watershed. The detailed soil survey report was completed for 12079 lakh hectares.

These surveys are utilised by Agriculture Forest Departments and other extension agencies. Reconnaissance survey was completed in 3.20 lakh hectares and report writing was done for 1.36 lakh hectares during the years 1978-79 to 1982-83.

(iv) Forest and Flora

Among the important trees found in the district are Dhonk, Babul, Kumtha, Khair, Reonjh, Kair, Hingot, Chilla, Papri, Khejra, Salar, Siras, Sisham, Rohira, Neem, Pipal, Phog, Aak, and Thor, etc. The main types of grass are Bharunt, Doob, Baru, Kaladhaman, Lapla and Munj, etc.

The forest area in Sikar district is not significant from the point of view of forest produce. Thorny and spiky bushes are found in the marginal lands, foothills and consolidated sandy plains or sand dunes and ravine lands. The Savannah type of vegetation is found in plains which are sandy or which contain sandy loam soils. This species is specially useful for grass production.

(v) Tne Use of Laud

The total geographical area of the district comes to 783909 hectares. The area for the purposes of land utilisation was

774924 hectares in 1983-84. The classification of land use in the district for the period 1983-84 is given in Table 2.3.

TABLE 2.3: **Classification of Land Use**

S. No.	*Name*	*Area*	*Percentage to Total Area*
1.	Forest	13363	1.72
2.	Land put to non-agricultural use	24852	3.21
3.	Barren and un-cultivated land	57131	7.37
4.	Other un-cultivated land excluding fallow land	48422	6.25
5.	Land under miscellaneous trees, orchards and groves	77	0.01
6.	Culturable waste	13951	1.80
7.	Fallow land	155418	20.06
8.	Net area sown	461710	59.58
			100.00

Source: Sankhikiya Rooprekha, Sikar, 1962. Directorate of Economics and Statistics, Rajasthan, Jaipur, pp. 66 to 68.

The above Table clearly reveals that the cultivable agriculture land covers the maximum area (59.58%) in the district and the second number goes to the barren land which is 7.9%

(*vi*) *Irrigation*

The district is what may be regarded as border line case with regard to the satisfactory agricultural conditions. In the absence of wide spread irrigational facilities, the suitability of the district with regard to normal agriculture has to be judged and justified in terms of the sufficiency or otherwise of rainfall. The areas getting an annual rainfall of less than 50 cms are generally not regarded as suitable for normal agriculture and Sikar district has an average rainfall of 460.9 mm with the result, they do not depend much on the monsoon rains. They go for man made sources of irrigation. The well system is one of them. So, wells are the fountain source of irrigation in the district, During 1983-84 the net irrigated area in the district was 107849 hectares of which 99.76 per cent was irrigated by means of wells and tube wells and the remaining 0.33 per cent by canals. The net ir rigated area constituted 19.80 per cent of the total net area sown during the year 1983-84.[4]

(*vii*) *The Crop Pattern*

The outstanding feature of the crop pattern in Sikar district is its wide variety of crops and abundance of food crops over non-food crops.

Kharif is the main crop of the district. Of the total area under different crops 85.66 per cent was utilised for cereals, 10.17 per cent for pulses and the rest 4.17 per cent for growing other crops during 1983-84. The important crops sown in the district in order of importance and preference are wheat, bajra, and gram. During 1983-84, it was wheat that covered 4.08 per cent of production whereas millet (bazra) yield was 13.31 per cent and gram was 2.14 per cent of the total production in the district.

(*viii*) *Tenancy*

Tenancy in the State is governed by Rajasthan Tenancy Act, 1955. It is one of the most important and progressive laws relating to the agrarian reforms. The provisions of the Act apply in respect of land held by tenants as if the State Government were the land holder acting through the Tehsildar in relation to land held by them. Every cultivator is either a tenant or a sub-tenant or an allottee or a trespasser. A tenant is one who is required to pay some rent on account of use and occupation of land let out to him for agricultural or allied purposes on a favourable rate of rent, *ijardar*, *thekedar* or trespasser is not considered a tenant.

There are various classes of tenants (a) Khatedar tenant (b) Maliks (c) Tenant of Khudkasht and (d) Ghair-Khatedar Tenant. A trespasser is a person who takes or retains possesison of land without authority. After regularisation, thc

4. *Techno-Economic Survey of Rajasthan*, National Council of Applied Economic Research, p. 18.

trespasser becomes an allottee. An allottee is treated as a Ghair Khatedar Tenant.

(*ix*) *Animal Husbandry*

According to the livestock Census 1977, the total livestock population of the district was 1361092 of which 20.29 per cent were cattle, 13.49 per cent buffaloes, 41.13 per cent goats, 21.63 per cent sheep, 0.04 per cent horses, 0.30 per cent donkeys, 2.95 per cent camels, 0.17 per cent pigs and a negligible percentage of mules. The poultry in the district numbered 7413 in 1977.

There were 12 veterinary hospitals, 4 veterinary health centres, 3 veterinary dispensaries and 2 mobile veterinary units in the district, in 1983-84. There were 9 Goshalas, 7 sheep extension centres and 3 sheep artificial insemination centres in the district in the year 1983-84.

With a view to preserving wild life from poaching and wanton killing the Rajasthan Wild Animals and Bird Protection Act 1951 was promulgated in 1952. In 1957, the forest rules were enforced in the district in order to protect wild life in forest areas.

(*x*) *Power*

The consumption pattern of electricity shows a fairly good use of power for agriculture purposes. The consumption of high voltage power is negligible, evidently because there are no large scale industries. In 1980-81, the domestic consumption of power in Sikar district was 3.225 million KWH, which rose to 7.666 million KWH in 1983-84. Other categories of electric consumption are public lighting, public water works, and irrigation, etc. Among these, a very significant rise has been marked in irrigation from 39.111 million KWH in 1980-81 to 134.480 million KWH in 1983-84. During 1980-81 the total consumption of electricity in the district was 37.414 million KWH which rose to 158.241 million KWH in 1983-84.

Under the desert development scheme eighty-four villages were electrified during 1983-84. Electric connections were given to 1832 wells and 32 Harijan basties were electrified on a primary basis during the year 1983-84.

(*xi*) *Industries and Labour*

Although there are no large scale industries in the district, yet due to favourable geographical situation regarding availability of raw material in huge quantity and it being the place of some of leading industrialists of the country, the district appears to have bright future for industrial development. Some of the important small scale industries are related to iron and steel fabrication, steel furniture, washing soap, ayurvedic medicines, oil and dal mills, polished cotton yarn, tie and dye and khadi and handloom cloths, etc.

There were 148 registered factories in the district during the year 1983-84. The district industrial centre registered 921 permanent and 569 proposed small scale units in the district with the help of Rajasthan Finance Corporation during the year 1983-84.

9022 persons were found registered with the Employment Exchange at the end of 1983 of which 7669 persons were registered during the year 1980 alone. There was a gradual increase in the number of persons getting themselves registered with the Employment Exchange from 1978 to 1983 but the number declined from 8113 in 1978 and 7669 in 1979. A similar trend of increase was observed in the number of persons registered with the Employment Exchange 9676 persons during the year 1983-84.

(*xii*) *Trade in Commerce*

The district is an exporter of industrial raw material besides foodgrains mainly wall, bajra, moth, moong, gawar, calcite powder, limestone, dolomite and quartz are exported from this district. Among the principal imports are foodgrain, sugar, construction material, industrial machinery, chemicals, textile, medicines and articles of general merchandise, etc.

There were 71 branches of various banks functioning in the district during 1983-84 of which 39 were functioning in the rural areas and 32 in the urban areas. All the tehsils and block headquarters are getting the advantage of banking facilities.

(*xiii*) *Transportation and Communication*

As far as the road transport is concerned, the district has a satisfactory network of all weather roads. Sikar is well connected with Jaipur, Delhi, Jodhpur, Bikaner by direct bus routes. All the block headquarters are linked with the district headquarter with pucca roads. Apart from one national highway, three State highways pass through the district. The total of 988 km length of roads comprises the national highway; 128 km painted road, 669 km mettled road, 69 km gravelled road, 67 km and fair weather and dressed up tracks 98 km in the district during the year 1983-84. Now the plans are under preparation for connecting villages with the population of 3000 to 4000 by roads.

With regard to the Post and Telegraph facilities, the district had 451 post offices, 18 telegraph offices and 13 telephone exchanges and 56 public call offices in the year 1983-84. All the blocks/tehsil headquarters are served by post, telegraph and telephone facilities.

The district is connected with the metre-gauge line of the Northern Railway. In all there are 26 railway stations in the district. All the important places of the district are connected with bus-routes. There are rest houses at Sikar, Reengus and Neem-ka-Thana.

(*xiv*) *Co-operative Movement*

The district had 531 co-operative societies of various types in 1983-84. There were one central co-operative bank, one primary land development (Mortgage) bank, 171 agricultural credit societies, 26 non-agricultural credit societies, 41 agricultural non-credit societies, and one central non-credit society. In all four Krishi Upaj Mandies existed at Sikar, Neem-ka-Thana Srimadhopur and Fatehpur during 1983-84.

The total membership of co-operative societies stood to 178780, share capital to Rs 128 lakhs and working capital to Rs 1042 lakhs during 1983-84. Loans worth Rs 463.95 lakhs were advanced during this period while recoveries made were of the order of Rs 373.55 lakhs and the loans due to remain to be recovered come to Rs 1044.81 lakhs.*

(*xv*) *Other Developmental Activities*

Under the Desert Development Programme, various

*Sankhikiya Rooprekha, Sikar, 1984, Directorate of Economics and Statistics, Rajasthan, Jaipur, p. 1162.

development schemes relating to animal husbandry, plantation, grazing ground, irrigation, rural electrification and dairy, etc. are in progress.

Under the small cultivators' development programme, loans amounting to Rs 725 lakhs were sanctioned to 148 persons for rearing of animals, to 252 to persons for agricultural work and 23 persons for providing irrigation facilities in the district during 1983-84. Under the training for rural youth under the self-employment scheme, the training was imparted to 374 persons.

Loans amounting to Rs 4.01 crores were distributed for economic development by the lead bank during 1983-84. Under the programme provision of drinking water facility in rural areas, hand pumps had been made available in 30 villages during 1983-84.

Under a Soil Conservation Scheme, a topographical survey has been carried out in 1095 hectares of land in the district and to provide irrigation facility. 25 sets were set-up in the fields under famine relief programme.

2. Population Pattern

The population of the Sikar district come to 13,77,245 as per 1981 Census of which 50.96 per cent were males and 49.04 per cent females. In all, 79.75 per cent of population resides in the rural areas and 20.25 per cent in urban areas. The rural portion of the district comprises 837 villages of which 813 are inhibited and the urban constitute 9 towns. Thus rural and urban population of Sikar district is 1098309 and 278936 respectively during the decade 1971-1981. Sikar district has recorded 32.08 per cent growth rate as compared to the growth rate of 32.97 per cent[5].

There are two important factors which determine the economic conditions of a region—human and physical—and these factors react upon each other. A study of human factor, its growth, composition and civil conditions, etc. is useful as it enables one to judge how far this factor has been instrumented in bringing the present economic condition in that region.

The population of Sikar district was 1377245 crores persons

5. Cap. A.D. Bannerman, *Census of India* (1901) Vol. XXV, B Rajputana, Part III, Lucknow, 1902, p. 19.

in 1981. This constituted 4.02 per cent of the total population of Rajasthan. It had a density of 178 persons per square kms. in the entire State of Rajasthan. Sikar district occupied the eleventh place in whole of Rajasthan in point of population, the first being held by Jaipur district.

(i) Growth of Population

Table 2.4 shows the variation in population in Sikar district during the past decade 1971-1981. Comparative figures of a few neighbouring districts have also been given. There has been an increase of +32.09 in the population of Sikar district as compared to +32.97 on the population of Rajasthan State as a whole.

The per cent increase in population in this district during 1971-1981 does not show any marked difference from that of the neighbouring districts. However when we consider that Sikar city during the past decade due to migration from other districts of Rajasthan must have been considerable the actual increase in the population of this district due to natural reasons should be considered lower than that recorded in the Table.

TABLE 2.4: **Variation in Population in Sikar District**

S. No.	*District/ Region*	*Population 1971*	*Population 1981*	*Variation (%)*
1.	Sikar	1042648	1377245	+32.09
2.	Jaipur	2482385	3420574	+37.91
3.	Churu	874439	1179466	+34.51
4.	Nagaur	1262155	1628669	+28.70
5.	Jhunjhunu	929230	1211583	+28.48
6.	Rajasthan	25765806	34261862	+32.97

Source: Census of India, 1977 Series I, Paper I, and Basic Statistics, Rajasthan, 1983, p. 38.

The population of Sikar city in 1971 was 70987 which rose to 102970 in 1981 recording an increase of +45.05 per cent. If we deduct the figure of Sikar city from the population figure of 1971 and 1981 Census, we will find that the population of Sikar district increased by only 23.7 per cent. Thus, the natural rate of growth of population of this district is lower than the rate of growth of population in Rajasthan.

(*ii*) *Rural and Urban Population*

A classification of population into rural and urban is important in so far as it indicates in several ways the stage of economic development out of a total population 1377245 in 1981. 278936 persons constituting 20.25 per cent of total population lived in urban areas of the district.

Table 2.5 shows that the rural population which constituted 865100 of the total population of Sikar district in 1971 increased to 1098309 in 1981. This clearly shows that the tendency of urbanisation is not marked in this district. If we study the comparative figures for Rajasthan State we will find that the urban population which formed 4543761 of the total population in 1971 increased to 7210508 in 1981. Thus it recorded an increase during the decade.

TABLE 2.5: **Variation in Rural and Urban Population (1971-1981)**

(*In 000*)

S. No.	*District*	*Urban*			*Rural*		
		1971	*1981*	*Increase/ Decrease %*	*1971*	*1981*	*Increase/ Decrease %*
1.	Sikar	178	279	56.74	865	1098	26.93
2.	Jaipur	746	1251	67.69	173	2170	1154.34
3.	Churu	259	345	33.20	616	834	35.38
4.	Nagaur	155	237	52.90	111	1392	1154.05
5.	Jhunjhunu	162	580	258.02	767	1088	41.58
6.	Rajasthan	454	721	58.81	212	270	27.35

Source: Statistical Abstract, p. 82, Census of India, 1981, Rajasthan Facts & Figures,

The urban population of Sikar district increased by 56.74 per cent as compared to 58.81 per cent in Rajasthan State. The percentage increase in the urban population in this district is higher than the increase in the neighbouring districts except Jaipur and Jhunjhunu. The urban population of Sikar district rose by 56.74 per cent during the past decade as compared to 58.81 per cent in Rajasthan State. The percentage increase in rural population of this district is lower than the percentage increase in other neighbouring districts.

(*iii*) *Sex Ratio*

No definite trend emerges as far as the sex ratio is concerned at the district level. The highest sex ratio was noted in 1981 and the lowest in 1901. Since 1901 the sex ratio has remained almost steady. In the rural areas the sex ratio has shown a steady rise since 1901 except in 1921 when it showed a decline. In the urban areas the sex ratio had shown a steady rise between 1931 and 1981 and since then it has been showing a steady increasing trend as is revealed from Table 2.6.

TABLE 2.6: **Sex Ratio Since 1901**

Census Year	*No. of Females per 1000 males*		
	Rural	*Urban*	*Total*
1901	854	996	877
1911	876	1016	899
1921	865	991	886
1931	896	994	913
1941	904	988	920
1951	955	1039	972
1961	957	996	964
1971	960	966	961
1981	965	922	963

Source: Census of India, Rajasthan Facts & Figures, p. 5.

As compared to 1971, sex ratio has shown slight increase in 1981 in the district at the district level in total and rural areas while a decline is to be noted in urban areas. The pattern has not been evenly followed in all the tehsils in total. Rural and urban areas and some tehsils have shown an increase in 1981 as compared to 1971 while others have shown a decrease as may be seen in Table 2.7.

TABLE 2.7: **Sex Ratio at Tehsils Level in 1971 and 1981**

District/Tehsil	*No. of Females as per 1000 Males*					
	1971			*1981*		
	Rural	*Urban*	*Total*	*Rural*	*Urban*	*Total*
Sikar (District)	960	966	961	965	952	963
Fatehpur (Tehsil)	974	1036	998	1024	1035	1029
Lachhmangarh (Tehsil)	997	1007	999	1016	969	1008
Sikar (Tehsil)	986	923	967	974	915	954
Neem-ka-Thana (Tehsil)	925	846	919	921	871	917
Srimadhopur (Tehsil)	946	977	949	943	918	939
Danta Ramgarh (Tehsil)	954	960	954	965	1002	967

Source: Census of India, 1981, Rajasthan Facts & Figures, p. 6.

The majority of males in population has not been reported only in this district but it is a feature of Rajasthan State as a whole. The fall in the female ratio is a matter of great concern. This will mean that more men will have to go without a partner in life. The increased facilities for maternity and child health the statutory grant of equality for the sexes, rise in the national and per capita income and the general economic welfare specially after independence, the sex ratio has not shown any signs of improvement.[6]

6. B.L. Lohia, *Rajasthan ki Jatiyan*, (Calcutta 1954), pp. 156-157.

(*iv*) *Occupational Structure and Economic Status Pattern*

The occupational structure in the rural areas of Sikar district does not exhibit any characteristic significantly different from the characteristic of the all India occupational pattern. As in the rest of the country agriculture is the main occupation of the rural majority of the people in this region. Out of a sample rural population of 1687 persons, no fewer than 1487 persons are dependent upon agriculture. In other words, 84.58 per cent of the rural population follows agriculture as the principal occupation.

Non-agriculture household constitute 16.93 per cent of the total rural household. Among the non-agricultural household 38.86 per cent have business and 29.65 per cent have labour as principal occupations. Only 1.51 per cent of the household depending chiefly upon agriculture have animal husbandry as a subsidiary occupation.

Assuming the rural working population to consist of males in the age group of 15-55 years (inclusive of both the limits) the total working force (excluding non-earning dependence) in the sample consisted of 507 persons out of this working force 432 persons are dependent primarily upon agriculture.

TABLE 2.8: **Occupation-Wise Population 1981**

Occupation	*Rural*	*Urban*	*Total*
(A) Total main workers	278393	60687	339080
(i) Cultivators	202665	6950	205615
(ii) Agriculture labour	13807	14917	1110
(iii) Household property industry, manufacturing, processing service and repairs	11069	4537	15582
(iv) Marginal workers	81113	4537	85650
(v) Other workers	50852	48114	98966
(B) Non-workers	738883	213712	952815

Source: Census of India, 1981, Rajasthan Facts and Figures, p. 7.

(*v*) *Literacy*

The literacy rates for total population, males and females, have shown a continuous increase since 1981. The literacy rate among females though has risen in the last thirty years and in 1981 it had become more than four times than that of 1951. It is still less than one-fourth of the males in 1981 and thus much remains wanting as far as female literacy is concerned. Table 2.9 presents the sex-wise literacy rates since 1951 as the district level as recorded during the past decade.

TABLE 2.9:: **Literacy Rates Since 1951**

Census	*Literacy Rates*		
	Males	*Females*	*Persons*
1951	13.53	2.06	2.89
1961	26.30	4.72	15.71
1971	32.15	6.57	19.61
1981	41.16	9.08	25.43

Source: Census of India 1981, Rajasthan Facts & Figures, p. 4.

The literacy rate among females is less than that of males in both rural and urban areas at the district and tehsil levels and it is also low among the females of the rural areas as compared to those of the urban areas. The highest literacy rate for the total population of males and females is to be observed in Sikar tehsil considering all areas.

At a glance Table 2.9 reveals that whereas 2.87 per cent of the population was lietrate in Sikar district in 1951, the percentage of literate persons rose to 25.43 per cent in 1981, recording an increase of 17.56 per cent. If a comparison is made with Rajasthan as a whole we find that the percentage of literate presons in the State was 19.07 per cent in 1971 which rose to 24.38 per cent in 1981 registering an increase of 5.31 per cent. Considering the literacy in Sikar district as a whole, it is found that the percentage of literate males and females which was 32.15 per cent and 6.57 per cent in 1971, rose to 41.16 per cent and 9.08 per cent respectively in 1981. In Rajasthan State as a whole the literacy among males and females rose from 28.74 per cent and 8.46 per cent in 1971 to 36.30 per cent and 11.42 per cent respectively in 1981. The performance of this district in the field of education has been better than that of the other neighbouring districts like Churu and Nagaur.

The literacy in the rural areas of the Sikar district in 1981 was as low as 22.43 per cent. Among rural females only 6.01 per cent were literate in 1981. However, the position was a little better in case of the rural males where the literacy per centage was 38.28 per cent. The low percentage of educated-females in rural areas is mainly marked because of a blind social belief among the rural people that a girl gets spoiled and unruly if she is allowed to go to school.

The highest literacy rate is observed in villages of higher population range in most of the tehsils. The highest literacy rate (29.98 per cent) has been observed in a village of Danta Ramgarh tehsil and the lowest (12.83 per cent) in the village of

TABLE 2.10: **Literacy Rates for Towns**

S. No.	*Name of Town*	*Literacy Rates (%)*
1.	Sikar (District)	37.23
2.	Fatehpur	33.19
3.	Khandela	27.44
4.	Lachhmangarh	36.81
5.	Losal	29.62
6.	Neem-ka-Thana	48.13
7.	Ramgarh	34.68
8.	Reengus	37.54
9.	Sikar	39,09
10.	Srimadhopur	46.05

Source: Census of India 1981, Rajasthan Facts and Figures, p. 8.

Meem-Ka-Thana tehsil.

The literacy rate among towns varies between 48.53 per cent in Neem-ka-Thana and 27.49 in Khandela. Only four towns out of nine, viz. Neem-ka-Thana, Srimadhopur, Sikar and Reengus known as higher literacy rates than the district average and the rest show a lower literacy rate than this average.

(*vi*) *Educational Facilities*

The number of various types of educational institutions in Sikar district in 1983-84 has been shown in Table 2.11 below.

TABLE 2.11: **Educational Institutions in Sikar District** (Year 1983-84)

S. No.	*Nature of Institution*	*No.*
1.	University	Nil
2.	Colleges for General Education	7
3.	Colleges for Special Education (Professional)	6
4.	High Schools and Higher Secondary Schools	119
5.	Middle Schools	216
6.	Junior Basic Schools	Nil
7.	Primary Schools	839
8.	Schools for Special Education	Nil
9.	Schools for Professional Education	9

Source: Sankhikiya Rooprekha, Sikar 1982, published by Directorate of Economics and Statistics, Rajasthan, Jaipur, p. 154.

Practically all institutions of higher learning are not situated in Sikar district. The total number of colleges of all types was thirteen. Thus there was one college for about 10594 persons and served an area of about 364 sq. kms. The total number of schools was 1177. There was thus one school for every 1170 persons and served an area of 113 sq. kms.

Let us examine the facilities for primary education in rural areas only out of 833 primary schools in the district. 506 schools in urban areas and 227 were in rural areas. The rural population in 1981 was 1098309 persons. Thus there was a primary school for about 3965 persons. Primary education as at present imparted is unproductive for literacy acquired under it has been lost before long and is not of any use to farmers in pursuing agriculture more efficiently. The basic system of education has widely been acclaimed as very useful as it aims at educating children in various types of crafts. The Government of Rajasthan is trying to convert primary schools into basic schools in a short period. Due to heavy financial implications, however, there are certain features of schools which can be easily introduced in the present primary schools. For example, the spirit of self-help and responsibility can be inculcated in children by entrusting them with small jobs. They should be taught to appreciate the beauty of nature and know about things in their environment such as flowers, insects and plants, etc. At present there is a great dearth of it in village schools and parrot like repetition of lessons goes on. The courses prescribed in schools should be such as may make rural children better farmers or better craftsmen and better men of sensibility.

At present the farmers do not send their children to schools as they help them in their fields and at homes by doing small odd jobs specially during the sowing and harvesting season. It is suggested that schools should be closed for about a fortnight or more during the sowing and harvesting seasons instead of summer months to enable the children to help their parents in fields. As the facility of primary education is not available in every village or Dhani also, children have to cover several miles to go to some other village where the school is located. In view of the bad state of village roads, the difficulty of even small distance is great especially in a bad weather. A primary school should be opened in every village or Dhani, so that this problem may be solved.

There is also shortage of equipment such as furniture, books, stationery, maps and materials for games, etc. in the village schools which hampers greatly the efficient performance of the teaching work. The need for proper school building and healthy surroundings is keenly felt practically everywhere. Further, the low salary of the primary school teacher does not give him much incentive to either stay in the profession or work with single-minded devotion.

Unless the defects pointed out above can be suitably removed, the Government cannot be deemed to have discharged its duties efficiently towards the future generation.

(*vii*) *Medical Facilities*

It is a well known fact that the medical facilities in rural areas of India are far from satisfactory. The conditions prevailing in rural areas of Sikar district are no exception to the general situation. In 1981 there were 9 hospitals with 453 beds, 26 dispensaries, one T.B. hospital and 8 child welfare maternity centres working in this district. Of these institutions, the big ones with adequate medical facilities are located in Sikar city. The Shree Kalyan hospital has 268 beds. Apart from the city the hospitals or dispensaries are situated either in tehsil headquarters or other important towns of the district. Only serious cases from nearby villages are taken to these for treatment.

The above discussion has brought us to the conclusion that it is Ayurvedic institutions rather than allopathic ones which serve the rural population of this district. They are scattered in rural areas. They have cheaper system of treatment and the medicine used can either be prepared at home or be cheaply had from the local shops. The allopathic institutions cater to the needs of urban population and have comparatively expensive medicines. It can now be safely said that the Government should increase the number of Ayurvedic institutions in rural areas and should provide more grant for medicine. The present facilities for treatment cannot be said to be satisfactory.

The number of beds in medical institutions per 1000 population comes to 2.33 at the district level and the highest such ratio is available at Sikar (3.21) and the lowest at Lachhmangarh (1.03) as may be seen from Table 2.12 giving number of beds in medical institutions per 1000 population in towns.

TABLE 2.12: **Number of Beds in Medical Institutions**

S. No.	*Class, Name and Civic Status of the Town*	*No. of Medical Institutions per 1000 Population*
1.	Sikar (District)	2.33
2.	Fatehpur (M)—II	2.56
3.	Khandela (M)—IV	1.27
4.	Lachhmangarh (M)—III	1.03
5.	Losal (M)—IV	2.11
6.	Neem-ka-Thana (M)—IV	2.36
7.	Ramgarh (M)—IV	1.12
8.	Sikar (M.C.I.)—I	3.21
9.	Srimadhopur (M)—IV	1.63
10.	Reengus	1.62

Source: Census of India 1981, Series 18, Rajasthan District Census Handbook, Sikar, p. vi.

(*viii*) *Working Population*

In the 1981 Census the population has been classified into three categories, viz. main workers, marginal workers, and non-workers on the basis of three economic activities. At the district level, 69.16 per cent of the population comprises non-workers, 24.62 per cent of workers, and the remaining 6.22 per cent of marginal workers. There is a lesser number of workers as well as marginal workers in urban areas as compared to rural areas both among males and females and there are main workers among males and compared to females. But marginal workers are more among females as compared to males in both urban as well as rural areas at the district as well as tehsil levels, as may be seen from Table 2.13.

The largest percentage of workers is engaged as cultivators at the district and tehsil levels in case of all areas and rural areas and as other workers in urban areas among both the sexes. A higher percentage of female workers is engaged in

TABLE 2.13: **Percentage of Workers, Marginal Workers and Non-Workers in the District (Year 1981-82)**

S. No.	*District/Tehsil*	*Total Rural Urban*	*Percentage of Main Workers to Total Population*			*Percentage of Marginal Workers to the Total Population*			*Percentage of Non-Workers to the Total Population*		
			Persons	*Male*	*Female*	*Persons*	*Male*	*Female*	*Persons*	*Male*	*Female*
1	2	3	4	5	6	7	8	9	10	11	12
1.	Sikar (D)	T	24.62	43.67	4.83	6.22	1.34	11.29	69.16	54.99	83.83
		R	25.35	44.56	5.44	7.38	1.53	13.45	67.27	53.91	81.11
		U	21.76	40.19	2.40	1.62	0.58	2.72	76.62	59.23	94.88
2.	Fatehpur (T)	T	23.67	48.86	6.95	5.13	1.39	8.78	71.20	57.75	84.27
		R	27.12	44.40	10.23	7.66	1.78	13.40	65.22	53.82	76.37
		U	18.89	35.93	2.43	1.64	0.84	2.42	79.47	63.23	95.15
3.	Lachhmangarh (T)	T	25.41	42.75	8.20	13.74	3.64	23.77	60.85	53.61	68.03
		R	26.39	43.67	9.38	15.66	4.12	27.01	57.95	52.21	63.61
		U	20.47	38.21	2.17	4.11	1.27	7.05	75.42	60.52	90.78
4.	Sikar (T)	T	24.82	44.52	4.16	4.40	0.97	7.99	70.78	54.51	87.85
		R	25.92	45.94	5.37	6.21	1.33	11.21	67.87	52.73	83.42
		U	22.54	41.70	1.60	0.69	0.26	1.16	76.77	58.04	97.24

(*Contd.*)

1	2	3	4	5	6	7	8	9	10	11	12
5.	Neem-ka-Thana (T)	T	23.92	43.05	3.06	4.25	0.87	7.93	71.83	56.08	89.01
		R	24.04	43.29	3.15	4.51	0.89	8.43	71.45	55.82	88.42
		U	22.29	40.10	1.84	0.98	0.66	1.35	76.73	59.24	96.81
6.	Srimadhopur (T)	T	24.00	43.81	2.00	5.55	0.77	10.64	70.45	55.42	86.46
		R	23.96	43.56	2.75	6.30	0.83	12.10	69.74	55.21	85.15
		U	24,22	43.00	3.94	1.42	0.44	2.49	74.36	56.56	93.77
7.	Danta Ramgarh (T)	T	26.06	45.79	5.65	6.43	1.27	11.77	67.51	52.94	82.58
		R	26.18	46.91	5.73	6.57	1.31	12.02	67.25	52.78	82.25
		U	24.32	44.08	4.59	4.58	0.73	8.43	71.10	55.19	86.98

Source: Census of India 1981, Series of Rajasthan District Census Handbook, Sikar, p. (xiviii).

cultivators as compared to male workers both in rural as well as urban areas and vice versa in case of other workers. As compared to males a larger percentage of workers among females is engaged in household industries in urban areas at both the district as well as tehsil levels except in tehsil Neem-ka-Thana where the position is reverse. A higher percentage of other workers is observed in urban areas as compared to rural areas and the percentage of other male workers is higher than the other female workers in both urban and rural areas of all the tehsils as may be seen from Table 2.14.

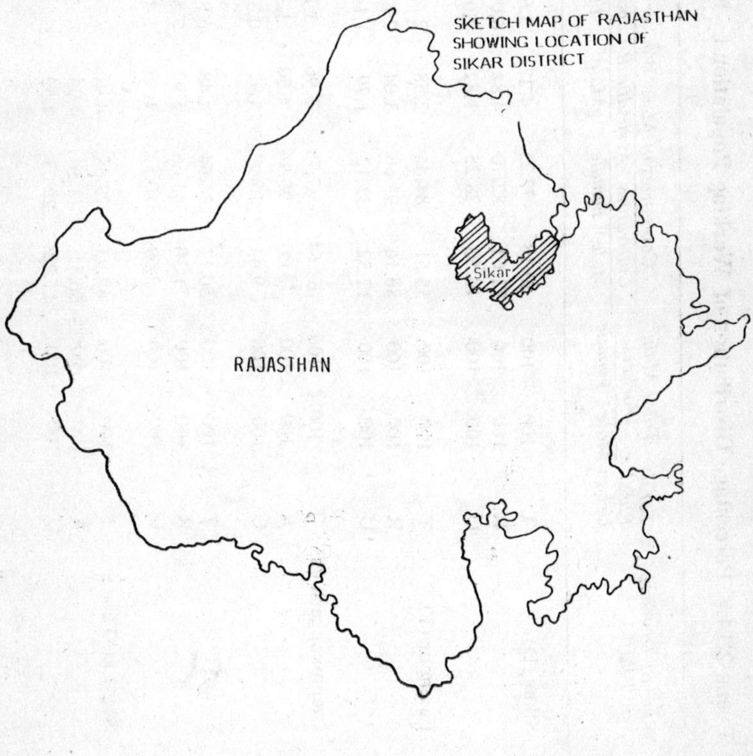

TABLE 2·14: **Percentage Distribution of Working Population by Economic Activity (Year 1981-82)**

S. No.	*Name of District/Tehsil*	*Total Rural Urban*	*Total Main Workers*		*Categories of Main Workers*				*Household Industry*		*Other Workers*	
					Cultivators		*Agricultural Labourers*					
			Male	*Female*	*Male*	*Female*	*Male*	*Female*	*Male*	*Female*	*Male*	*Female*
1.	Sikar (D)	T	100	100	60.18	77.25	4.27	5.60	4.53	5.24	31.02	11.91
		R	100	100	71.63	82.70	4.84	6.00	4.05	3.31	19.49	7.99
		U	100	100	10.50	28.25	1.82	2.02	6.57	2.62	81.11	47.11
2.	Fatehpur (T)	T	100	100	55.51	84.44	2.58	2.63	2.55	4.13	35.86	8.80
		R	100	100	86.16	93.66	3.04	2.88	1.23	2.39	9.57	1.07
		U	100	100	12.32	31.12	1.79	1.14	4.81	14.19	81.08	53.55
3.	Lachhmangarh (T)	T	100	100	67.64	87.78	3.96	3.18	2.88	4.38	25.52	4.66
		R	100	100	78.00	90.96	4.50	3.31	2.34	2.33	15.16	3.40
		U	100	100	9.44	16.99	3.97	0.32	8.89	50.00	83.70	32.69
4.	Sikar (T)	T	100	100	50.13	74.64	4.48	6.82	4.03	4.29	41.36	14.25
		R	100	100	71.30	83.66	5.92	7.56	3.41	1.75	19.37	7.03
		U	100	100	3.59	10.53	1.30	1.52	5.40	22.34	89.71	65.61
5.	Neem-ka-Thana	T	100	100	62.93	79.68	4.91	7.26	4.11	5.23	29.05	15 83
		R	100	100	66.81	73.56	4.93	7.52	4.08	5.36	24.18	10.56
		U	100	100	11.22	29.77	4.52	1.53	4.50	2.29	79.71	66.41

6.	Srimadhopur (T)	T	100	100	61.18	58.97	4.20	8.99	5.14	22.72	27.41	19.32
		R	100	100	70.40	65.28	4.50	10.22	5.09	8.50	20.01	16.00
		U	100	100	16.60	33.06	2.53	3.05	11.06	30.06	68.48	32.93
7.	Danta Ramgarh	T	100	100	64.63	75.94	4.88	6.97	6.06	2.99	24.43	14.10
		R	100	100	66.81	76.84	5.08	7.24	5.97	2.63	22.14	13.29
		U	100	100	33.41	61.16	2.01	2.45	7.37	8.87	57.21	27.52

Source: Census of India 1981, Series 18 Rajasthan District Census Handbook, Sikar p. (*x*iix).

3

Land Utilisation and Crop Pattern

The well being of agricultural population depends upon land and its proper use. The study of land utilisation provides an opportunity to find out if the land of a certain tract or region has been properly utilised or if there has been a lopsided development which needs readjustment from the point of view of land use capability[1]. The systematic exploitation of primary resources is the *sine-qua-non* of a planned economy. India has adopted planning as the core of her official policy and the development of our country has in recent years undergone various changes. It is useful to study the land utilisation pattern of this district.

1. Land Use Pattern

The land use pattern has been presented under the five headings :

(*i*) *Forest*

Forest is the land which has been declared as forest by the competent authority. The total area of the forest in Sikar district 1970-71 was 12351 hectares. It increased to 14059 hectares in 1983-84. A notable feature of the forest figures during the planning period is the unexpected change in it from year to year.

A general conclusion can well be drawn that the area under

1. P.T. George, *Ceilings on Landholdings in India,* Review National Institute of Rural Development (Hyderabad 1979), p. 318.

DIAGRAM SHOWING PERCENTAGE OF LAND USE PATTERN

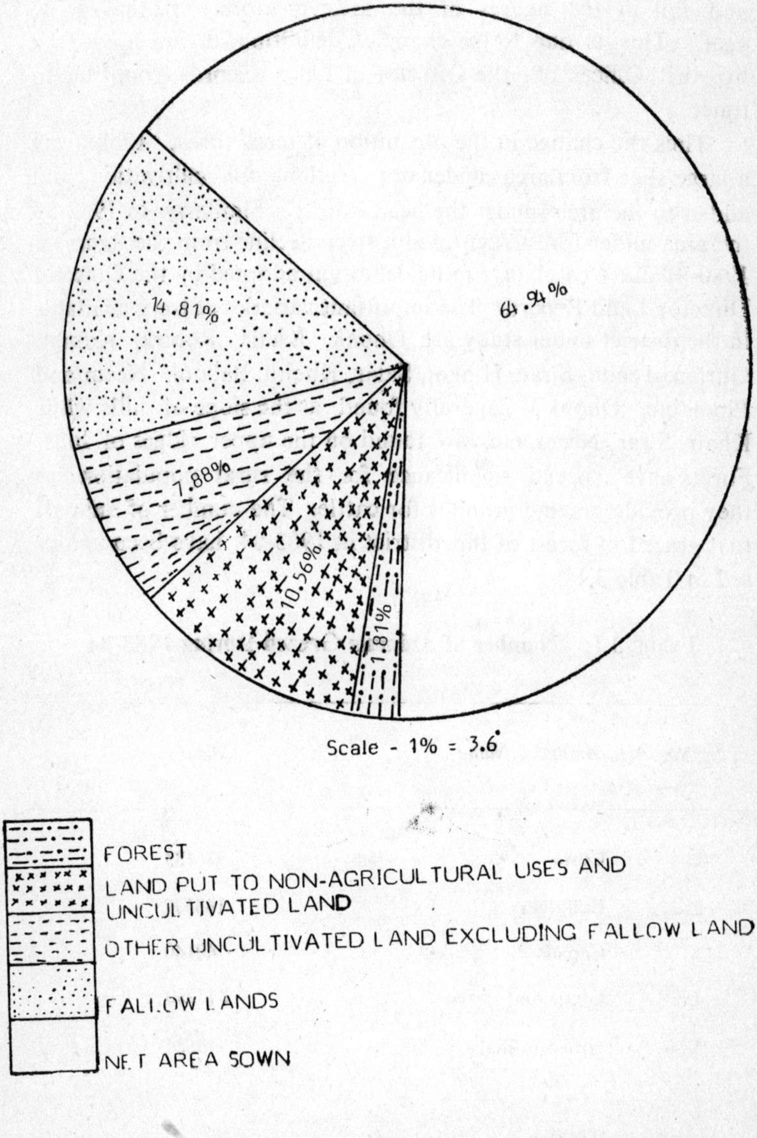

forest declined during the span of the two plan periods. The question that remains to be explained is the sudden rise and fall in the figures of the area of forest from year to year. This is due to the changing definition of forest adopted by the Office of the Director of Land Records from time to time.

Thus the change in the definition of term 'forest' took away a large slice from area under not available for cultivation and added to the area under the head 'forest'. Similarly in 1982-83 the area under forest registered a steep decline from the figure of 1980-81 due to a change in its definition adopted by the Office of Director Land Records. The important varieties of trees available in the district under study are Dhonk, Khair, Rohira, Kumat, Gurjan, Tendu, Sirar, Hingot, Salar, Khejra, Babool, Neem and Pipol, etc. Dhonk is ganerally found at the slope of hills while Khair, Sirar, Neem, etc. are found on the upper ridges of hills. Forets have special significance for the rural population as they provide grazing grounds for cattle. The number of animals that grazed in forest of this district in 1983-84 have been analysed in Table 3.1

TABLE 3.1: **Number of Animals Grazed During 1983-84**

S. No.	*Animals' Name*	*Mumber*
1.	Cows	276183
2.	Buffaloes	183572
3.	Camels	40140
4.	Goats and sheep	848230
5.	Other animals	40634
	Total	1388759

Source : Sankhikiya Rooprekha, Sikar, 1984, Directorate of Economics and Statistics, Rajasthan, Jaipur, p. 85.

During the days of old Sikar *Thikana*, grazing of animals was allowed free of charge in forest. But now free grazing is not allowed in the reserved forest areas. Cultivators are required to pay the grazing fee on the basis of kind and number of animals grazed. The important varieties of grass grown in this district are Bharoot or Bhurat, Anjan, Surwala, Gandhel and Gwan, while the first four varieties are generally grown in plains, the last is grown in hilly areas.

(*ii*) *Expansion of Forest*

The need for improvement of forests and expansion of areas under them can hardly be overemphasised. Judicious afforestation has widely been acclaimed as the most potent weapon against soil erosion. The forest policy resolution suggests a forest cover of 60 per cent of the area in hilly regions and 20 per cent in plains. On this basis, the area under forest in this district should be much more than what it is today. The main difficulty in expansion of forests in this district is scarcity of water. The rural population has also been sometimes found to be averse to such expansion due to damage to life and crops caused by wild animals living in these forests.

However, the forest should be expanded and the best way in our opinion is the creation of farm forest. The main object of such expansion is to make the farmers self-sufficient in the matter of fuel and timber requirements. Such a system of raising trees provide cultivators a second line of defence against crop failures. The less apparent but the more important advantage of farm forests is that they bring the soil conservation method rights in the midst of field by providing wind breakers embankments and soil nutrients. They also provide fodder for animals and are quite common in foreign countries.

At present large blocks of land are lying as the waste land in rural areas in the name of pasture lands but virtually these grow nothing. Such areas may also be taken up from growing grass and plantation of trees to provide fodder and shade to the cattle. Special attention should be paid to grow commercial timber instead of only firewood. This will help the cultivators economically and enrich the district, such trees would also serve as a nucleus for many industries in future.

(*iii*) *Other Uncultivated Land Excluding Fallow Land*

Other uncultivated land excluding the fallow land comprises three sub-heads:

(i) Permanent pastures and other grazing lands;
(ii) Land under tree crops and groves not included in the net area sown; and
(iii) Cultivable waste (i.e. land which may either be fallow or covered with shrubs and jungles).

TABLE 3.2: **Distribution of Other Uncultivated Land Under Three Heads Hectares**

Head	*1970-71*	*1983-84*	*Increase* (+) *Decrease* (—) %
(a) Permanent pasture and grazing land, etc.	48610	48857	(+) 0.50
(b) Land under tree crops and groves, etc.	49	81	(+) 65.30
(c) Cultivable waste	13594	12655	(—) 6.90

S*ource*: Sankhikiya Rooprekha, Sikar, 1984, Directorate of Economics and Statistics, Rajasthan, Jaipur, p. 68.

The area under permanent pastures and other grazing lands increased steadily from year to year. The average land under tree crops and groves also showed a growing tendency during the planning period. Land under tree crops and groves is certainly a very welcome and encouraging trend.

The fall in the area of 'cultivable waste' show that more land has been brought under cultivation or has been utilised for pastures or other groves.

However, it is true that a part of the land classed as cultivable waste may be practically uncultivable. A part of it may be covered by shrubs or infested by weeds, some may be cut up into ravines by soil erosion and some may be water logged or salline. As indicated by the Ministry of Agriculture, Government of India, it appears that some fallow land may be brought under cultivation. There cannot be much justification in keeping these lands or even a part of them uncultivated for long.

(*iv*) *Fallow Land*

Fallow land can be divided under the following two heads;

(a) Current Fallow, and
(b) Other Fallow.

(*a*) *Current Fallow*: Current fallow land is the land which is kept unucltivated for a period of one year or less than five years. The main purpose of keeping land fallow is to enable it to reocup its fertility of which it is lost by repeated raising of crops on it. In this region dry cultivation is practised over more than 70 per cent of the area. As the rich elements of manure cannot be assimilated in soil due to paucity of water, lands have to be left fallow can be abandoned to a very great extent if more irrigational facilities become available and scientific crop rotation is adopted. There are some catch-cum-cover crops like cowpea, plures, instead of leaving land fallow. Technical improvement and research have now reduced the necessity of leaving land fallow. It is generally said that in Western countries the practice of fallow land has been replaced by inter filled row crops like potatoes and roats, etc. which help the soil to recoup its fertility. The necessity of leaving land uncultivated is now to be advisable only under special circumstances only in conditions of extreme drought.

(*b*) *Othev Fallow Land*: Other fallow lands are those lands which are left uncultivated for a period exceeding one year but less than five years. The reason for keeping these lands fallow for such long periods are many and varied. Some of the important causes are poverty of cultivators, inadequate supply of water, silting up of canals and rivers, unremunerative nature of farming or even feat that if land is let out to tenants, they may acquire permanent rights.

The area under other fallow lands was 36036 hectares in 1980-81. It increased to 48115 hectares in 1983-84 which formed 8.30 per cent to the total area sown. The reasons for keeping lands fallow have been briefly discussed earlier. Apart from this, the causes have either been removed or are being removed with the advancement in Science and Agricultural Chemistry and soil technology. It can, therefore, be safely expected that a major portion of fallow land can be brought under cultivation with the help of modern scientific methods of agriculture and increase in irrigation facilities.

The distribution of fallow lands with percentage to total area sown has been shown in Table 3.3.

TABLE 3.3: **Distribution of Fallow Lands with Percentage to Total Area Sown**

(Hectares)

Year	*Current Fallow Land*	*Percentage to Total Area Sown*	*Other Fallow Land*	*Percentage to Total Area Sown*
1980-81	88675	16.65	36036	6.75
1981-82	74256	13.50	45583	8.29
1982-83	100802	19.57	54616	10.60
1983-84	66441	11.47	48115	8.30

Source: Sankhiya Rooprekha, Sikar, 1984, Directorate of Economics and Statistics, Rajasthan, Jaipur, p. 69.

The above Table makes it clear that at least a part of the vast stretches lying as current fallow could be brought under the plough by adopting scientific agricultural methods.

(*v*) *Net Area Sown*

In 1980-81 the area under this head was 493878 hectares which showed an upward trend. There was a sharp increase in it during 1983-84 and it increased to 5232270 hectares. This increase in the net area sown represents a growth of 82.15 per cent.

Area Sown More Than Once: The area sown more than once increased from 38625 hectares in 1980-81 to 69860 hectares in

1983-84, i.e. there was an increase of 33951 hectares or 94.54 per cent. This phenomenal increase was due to the efforts of the Government to achieve self-sufficiency in food production during the plan period.

Looking to the extension of irrigation facilities and community development programmes in the rural areas, one feels that the changes in land utilisation pattern could be much better. The initial state of planning period had not been quite satisfactory but now the performance of land utilisation pattern is still better due to modern agriculture techniques being used by the farmers.

TABLE 3.4: **Land Utilisation Pattern**

(Hectares)

Year	*Net Area Sown*	*Area More than Once*	*Total Area Sown*
1980-81	493878	38625	532503
1981-82	497610	52144	549754
1982-83	461710	53162	514872
1983-84	523270	69860	579130

Source : Sankhikiya Rooprekha, Sikar, 1984, Directorate of Economics and Statistics, Rajasthan, Jaipur, p. 70.

From Table 3.4 it is clear that there has been an increasing tendency in the net area sown, area sown more than once and the total area as well. It is quite satisfactory so far as the land use pattern is concerned.

2. Crop Pattern

In order to obtain a comprehensive idea of the economic use of land, the study of land utilisation has to be pursued with reference to the allocation of land for the cultivation of various crops. The choice as well as the combination of crops in any region is conditioned by the climatic factors. Nevertheless, the returns from land can be considerably augmented bya planned selection of crops and scientific methods of a crop-rotation.[2]

The outstanding feature of crop pattern in Sikar district is its wide variety of crops and predominance of food crops over non-food crops. In this chapter an attempt has been made to study the acreage production and average yield of the main food and non-food crops during the year 1983-84. For an analytical study, crops have been broadly classified under five heads:

(i) Cereals
(ii) Pulses
(iii) Sugarcane
(iv) Cotton, and
(v) Oil seeds

(Gram has been included under the head 'cereals' for the present study.)

(*a*) *Cereal*

Among cereals, the only other important crop is wheat, occupying sown 34929 hectares and having a production of 69418 million tonnes in 1983-84. The average turn out was 931 per hectares in the year 1983-84.

(*i*) *Wheat*: Wheat needs soil preparation like that for barley. The period for sowing and interculture are also the same but irrigation is more frequent, up to seven waterings may be needed for areas served by wells. The crop is ready for hervest between 10th of April and 15th of May. The production of wheat went up sharply from 25045 million tonnes in 1980-81, to 69418 million tonnes in 1983-84. Showing an increase of 44373 million tonnes. The production of wheat in 1980-81 was 1.39 million tonnes per hectare. It rose to 2.00 million tonnes in 1983-84 The increase in the total production of wheat during 1980-83 may be attributed to increase in the land available as well as the per hectares rise in production. The contribution of wheat in Rajasthan's total cereals production was 2.35 per cent during the year 1983-84.

---

2. The entire chapter is based on official statistics released by the Land Records Office Govt. of Rajasthan,

(*ii*) *Barley*: This crop is next in importance to bajra among food grains with regard to the area available for cultivation. An area of 19942 hectares was devoted to barley cultivation out of the total area available to all cereals and millets of about 3 lakhs hectares in 1983-84.

Barley exhibits a wide ecological adaptation. It is generally grown on light soils. It needs a more bed than wheat but can tolerate alkalinity. Tillage and soil preparation is done twice, first from 20th April to 10th May and then from 10th September to 15th November. During the latter operation, the soil is prepared for sowing, which is done from the fourth week of October to mid-December. The fields are generally watered four times. First at the time of sowing and then at the beginning of January, middle of February, and then beginning of March. The period for interculture lasts for the whole of January. Harvesting is done between late March and mid-April.

Fatehpur and Lachhmangarh tehsils were insignificant for barley cultivation. The largest contribution comes from Srimadhopur followed by Danta Ramgarh and Neem-ka-Thana. Sikar had small area for barley. The trend of production of barley showed a continuous decrease throughout the period. Production of this crop went down from 32517 million tonnes in 1980-81 to 27712 million tonnes in 1983-84 indicating a decrease of 4805 millions tonnes or 14.77 per cent. The production per hectare of barley in 1980-81 was 2.14 million tonnes. It decreased to 1.59 million tonnes in 1983-84. The contribution of barley production in Rajasthan's cereals production was 4.75 per cent in the year 1983-84.

(*iii*) *Gram*: Gram was grown on 22143 hectares in 1983-84, which gave a turnout of 37454 million tonnes. This is the only Rabi pulse of the district. Summer ploughing for the crop is done between the fourth weak of April and the second weak of May. Preparation of soil for sowing is done between 25th September and 15th October. The actual sowing is done between 15th and 20th October. The harvesting period lasts from the second week of March to the second week of April. The tehsils where gram was grown were Neem-ka-Thana, Srimadhopur, Danta Ramgarh and Sikar. In 1980-81 the production of gram was 24466 million tonnes which increased to 37454 million tonnes in 1983-84 showing an increase of 12988 million tonnes at the entire period of four years ended as 1983-84. The production per hectares of gram in 1983-84 was 2.91 million tonnes. Thus we can say that the increase in production of gram was the cumulative effect of increased hectars and higher yield per hectare. The contribution of gram production in Rajasthan's cereals production is 3.00 per cent in the year 1983-84.

(*iv*) *Bajra*: This crop accounts for the bulk production area under food grains. In 1983-84, 254627 hectares were devoted to the cultivation of bajra. It is one of the most important millet crops and is put to multiple uses. The flour is used for chapati and forms a major part of the daily food of the masses. It can also be taken as fried. It is a crop of low rainfall areas and welcomes bright sunshines after light showers during the growth period. Heavy rain is disastrous to it. Bajra is generally sown on the proper type of soils and can be sown either mixed or alone. The fields are prepared by repeated ploughings after the first fall of rains. Tillage and soil preparation are done from the end of March to the end of April and the sowing periods are from late June to late July. The crop is not irrigated. Interculture is done from the third week of August to mid September. The crop is harvested in September or October and thrashing is done after Rabi crop sowing. The principal bajra producing tehsils are Sikar, followed by Lachhmangarh, Danta Ramgarh, Fatehpur, Srimadhopur and Neem-ka-Thana. The production of bajra was 81019 million tonnes during 1980-81 which decreased to 24348 million tonnes in 1983-84. Thus there was a decrease of 56671 million tonnes during the year 1983. The production per hectare was 0.670 million tonnes. The contribution of bajra production in Rajasthan's total cereals production was 10.08 per cent during the year 1983-84.

(*v*) *Maize*: In 1980-81 the hectares under maize was 363 hectares which constituted 0.14 per cent of the total cropped area. In 1983-84 it decreased to 324 hectares and constituted 0.10 per cent of the total cropped area. To sum up, it can be said that from 1980-81 to 1983-84 maize crop constitute a significant decrease from the hectares point of view. The production of maize in 1980-81 was 179 million tonnes. It decreased to 85 million tonnes in 1983-84. Thus during the year there was a decrease of 94 million tonnes. The production per hectare of maize in 1983-84 was 0.26 million tonnes. The contribution of maize production in Rajasthan's cereals production is 1.13 per cent in the year 1983-84.

(*vi*) *Jowar*: In 1980-81, the area under jowar was 184 hectares. The area increased to 269 hectares in 1983-84. The net increase over these years was 85 hectares. The production of jowar in 1980-81 was 58 million tonnes. It decreased to 49 million tonnes in 1983-84, registering a fall of 9 million tonnes or 15.52 per cent. The production per hectare of jowar in 1983-84 was 0.18 million tonnes. The decrease in production of jowar was due to decline in hectares accompanied by a fall in per acre yield.

(*vii*) *Rice*: In 1980-81 the area under rice was only 68 hectares. In 1981-82 the area increased to 209 hectares but in 1983-84 the area decreased to 26 hectares. The production of rice in 1980-81 was 91 million tonnes but in 1983-84 it decreased to 1 million tonne. This is not good for cereals. The production per hectare of rice in 1983-84 was 0.03 million tonnes.

(b) *Pulses*

(*i*) *Rabi Pulses*: In 1980-81, the area under Rabi pulses was 5909 hectares. It increased to 12843 in 1983-84 over these years. The area increased to 6934 hectares or constituted 117.34 per cent. The production of Rabi pulses rose from 24491 million tonnes in 1980-81 to 39080 million tonnes in 1983-84 showing an increase of 14589 million tonnes. The production per hectare of pulses (Rabi) in 1983-84 was 3.04 million tonnes.

(*ii*) *Kharif Pulses*: In 1980-81, the area under Kharif pulses was 160354 hectares constituting 39.7 per cent of the total cropped area. It decreased to 124234 hectares (by 22.52 per cent) in 1983-84. The production of Kharif pulses was 38389 million tonnes in 1980-81 which increased to 39200 million tonnes in 1983-84. During the period 1980-1983, the production increased by 811 million tonnes or constituting 2.11 per cent. The average annual production of Kharif pulses during these years showed the increasing trend.

(*c*) *Sugarcane*

In 1980-81, the area under cultivation for sugarcane was 75 hectares (0.10 per cent of the total cropped area) which increased to 81 hectares in 1983-84. In 1980-81, the production of sugarcane was 3381 million tonnes which increased to 3669 million tonnes in 1983-84. Showing an increase of 288 million tonnes (8.51 per cent). The average annual production of sugarcane during 1980-83 was 45080 kg. per hectare. In contribution of sugarcane production in Rajasthan's total sugarcane production is 0.26 per cent in the year 1983-84.

(*d*) *Cotton*

In 1980-81, the area under cotton cultivation was 1 hectare which increased to 24 hectares in 1983-84. constituting 4.3 per cent of the entire period of four years. The area under cotton showed a steep increase in 1982 when it came to 18 hectares from 5 hectares in 1981. In 1980-81, the production of cotton was one bale which increased to 84 bales in 1983-84. However, it took a good turn during this period, both the area and production increased.

(*e*) *Oilseeds*

(*i*) *Groundnut*: The only other important commercial crop of the district is groundnut sown on 3974 hectares in 1983-84. The production of the crop was 2662 tonnes. The tillage and soil preparation of groundnut is done during the month of April. With the fall of the regular monsoon, i.e. the end of the June or the beginning of July, preparation is made for sowing which is actually done between 10th July and 15th August. Irrigation is not required and interculture is done during October. By october end, the crop is harvested. The production of groundnut decreased from 1653 million tonnes in 1980-81 to 66 million tonnes in 1983-84. The average yield of the crop in 1983-84 was 400 kg. per hectare. The decline in production is due to fall in the average land used.

(*ii*) *Rape and Mustard*: This class of the oil seeds had the largest area among commercial crops, the figures being 8493 hectares and production 679 tonnes in 1983-84. This is also a Rabi season crop and as such tillage and soil preparation are the same as gram. The sowing is done between mid-October and mid-November, Cultivation is mostly combined with wheat or barley. Interculture is done between 15th December and 30th January. The harvesting of mustard is done from 15th March to 30th March and in February. The various tehsils having significant areas under the crop were Neem-ka-Thana and Srimadhopur tehsils. The production was 679 tonnes in 1983-84. The average production of the crop was 300 kg. per hectare in 1983-84. The contribution of Rape and Mustard oilseeds production in Rajasthan's oilseeds production is 0.15 per cent in the year 1983-84.

3. Review Progress of Scientific Agriculture

One of the important functions of the Agriculture Department is to motivate the farmers for adoption of better farming techniques and to educate them in the use of scientific means of agriculture. There is a constant and extensive effort for introducing better implements, seeds and chemical fertilizers, etc.[3,4]

(*i*) *Improved Implements*

The improved implements being distributed in the district are better ploughs, chaff cutters and seed drills.

Indication of the progress of mechanisation of agriculture is provided by the increasing use of the tractor. At the time of 1971 Census of agriculture implements and machinery, there were 24 tractors in the district. This number rose to 451 in 1984.

3. Issac Arnon, Modernisation of Agriculture in Developing Countries, Jhon Willy & Sons, 1981.
4. Theodor Bergmann, Mechanisation of Indian Farming, Obstacles and Prospects, Popular Prakashan, Bombay, 1978.

TABLE 3.5: **Important Implements in District**

(*Number*)

S. No.	*Name of Implements*	*1980-81*	*1981-82*	*1982-83*	*1983-84*
1.	Improved ploughs	335	658	640	451
2.	Chaff cutters	73	143	324	229
3.	Seed drills	—	48	112	3
4.	Others	400	620	45	287

Source : Sankhikiya Rooprekha, Sikar, 1983, Directorate of Economics and Statistics, Rajasthan, Jaipur, p. 64.

(*ii*) *Improved Seeds*

The cultivators are now realising the importance of the hybrid seeds which have given considerable improvement in crop yield as compared to the old conventional varieties. This is due to the adoption of hybrid bajra, the yield had gone up to 50 to 60 per cent in case of wheat also which is the major Rabi cereal, the adoption of the maxican seed had given a similar increase in output. The varieties of bajra are HB-I and HB-3 and those of wheat are Kalyana Sona, Sonalika R-R 21 Lal Bahadur, etc.

As a part of popularisation drive for the high yielding variety, the cultivators are contacted personally and the benefits of the new strain are explained to them. There are some special development schemes also in force.

(*iii*) *Seed Multiplication*

There is departmental multiplication farm at Reengus in Srimadhopur tehsil. The farm has an area of 135 acre and the equipment includes a tractor and electric pumping set. Cultivation on the farm is done on scientific lines and consequently chemical fertilizers are used. The consumption of such fertilizers at the farm has been shown in Table 3.6.

While going through the Table, it is clear that consumption of fertilizers is showing an increasing trend after the year 1980-81.

TABLE 3.6: **Consumption of Fertilisers**

Years	*Consumption (Quantity—Kg.)*
1980-81	3100
1981-82	150
1982-83	1100
1983-84	1700

Source : Office of the District Agriculture Officer, Sikar, 1984.

It is good for the economy of the district to a large extent.

(*iv*) *Fertilizer Scheme*

Under this scheme, fertilizer distribution is done through the co-operative societies and private dealers. The figures of distribution of various types of fertiliser have been shown in Table 3.7.

TABLE 3.7 : **Distribution of Various Types of Fertilisers**

(*Tonnes*)

S. No.	*Types of Fertilisers*	*1981-82*	*1982-83*	*1983-84*
1.	Nitrogenous	428	379	1044
2.	Phosphatic	38	48	66
3.	Potassic	2.5	15	19
	Total	468.5	442	1127

Source: Office of the District Agriculture Officer, Sikar, 1984.

While going through the Table, it is clear that consumption of Nitrogenous types of fertiliser is steeply increased rather than other types of fertilisers, because this type of fertiliser is fit for the district's soil.

(*v*) *Fruit Development Schemes*

The Panchayat Samities are popularising fruit plantation in their respective areas and as such the district agriculture Office collects their requirements and supplies the requisite number of plants. The cultivators are provided technical guidance on the development of orchards by the Agriculture Assistant. The progress of the scheme is shown in Table 3.8.

TABLE 3.8: **Progress of Fruit Development Scheme**

S. No.	*Types of Work*	*Units*	*1981*	*1982*	*1983*
1.	Fruit plant distribution	No	3471.0	7618.0	8656.0
2.	Plantation of new orchards	Hectares	0.5	2.0	3.0
3,	Rejuvenation of old orchards	,,	2.0	2.5	3.0
4.	Grape cultivation	,,	44.0	4.0	1.2

Source: Sankhikiya Rooprekha, Sikar, 1981, Directorate of Economics and Statistics, Rajasthan, Jaipur, p. 77.

While going through the Table, it is clear that the distribution of fruit plant was the maximum in the year 1983-84. But grapes cultivation is not going on good direction due to soil conditions of the district.

(*vi*) *Oilseed Scheme*

During 1970 to 1983, 25 demonstrations were carried out in sunflower cultivation in the Kharif season and a similar number of demonstrations in the Rabi season were conducted for mustard. A scheme for sunflower cultivation has been in force since 1971 and that for mustard was started in 1983-84 each demonstration plot is of the size of one acre.

(*vii*) *Rotation of Crops*

The district is largely a single crop area, but on lands which are irrigated by wells, the high yielding varieties are also used. In such cases one year rotation is followed which is like this. Hybrid bajra plus moong moth followed by wheat.

4. Irrigation

The district is what may be regarded as a border line case with regard to satisfactory agricultures conditions. In the absence of wide spread irrigational facilities, the districts's suitability with regard to normal agriculture has to be judged, in terms of sufficiency or otherwise of rainfall. Areas getting an annual rainfall of less than 50 cms. are generally not regarded as suitable for normal agriculture[5] and Sikar district has an average rainfall of 460.9 mm.

The prosperity of agriculturist of any region depends on how far the irrigation system has developed in that region. There is no large scale canal facility in Sikar district and agriculture depends mainly on wells, tanks, tube wells and such other sources.

TABLE 3.9: **Irrigation by Sources during the Last 5 Years**

(*Hectares*)

Year	*Canal*	*Percentage to Total net Irrigated Area*	*Tank*	*Percentage to Total Irrigated Area*	*Wells and Tube Wells*	*Percentage to Total Irrigated Area*	*Total net Irrigated Area*
1980-81	699	1.34	850	0.16	51296	98.49	52080
1981-82	388	0.67	261	0.45	56619	98.86	57268
1982-83	509	0.72	224	0.31	69292	98.95	70025
1983-84	350	0.32	—	—	107499	99.67	107849

Source: Statistical Abstract, Rajasthan, Volume for Various Years, 1980 to 1984.

5. *Techno Economic Survey of Rajasrhan*, National Council of Applied Economic Research, p. 18,

The underground water level shows a large variation due to the varied configuration of the tract. The water level varies from 5 metres to 20 metres in eastern parts and 30 to 40 metres in the western parts.

(*a*) *Irrigation by Sources*

(*i*) *Wells*: As wells are the prime source of irrigation in this district, it is very necessary that new wells should be added and old wells be kept in a proper state of repair so that irrigation work may not suffer. The only important sources which remain to be utilised by cultivators for purpose of irrigation are the wells, rivers and streams.

There are no perennial rivers in the district. However, there are some seasonal streams notably the Kantli, Mendha, Dohan, and the Sabi, etc. They are of no great use for irrigation purpose as such there is not much irrigation by canals. Similarly, tank irrigation is not taken to any significant scale.

While going through the Table, it is clear that wells and tube wells are the most important source of irrigation in this district. About 98 per cent to 99 per cent of the net area is being irrigated by this source. Contribution of canals and tanks is equivalent to nil.

The number of electrical operated wells in the district stood at 14370 at the end of the year 1983-84. The year-wise position of the wells energised during the last four years ending 1983-84 is shown in Table 3.10.

While going through the Table, it is clear that the increase in area under wells irrigation cannot be said to be encouraging because it was only about one per cent per year. In case of irrigation by means of wells, the progress regarded somewhat better but not up to the mark. Greater attention should have been paid to bring more land under wells irrigation. This could be possible by digging new wells on a much larger scale than was done and by utilising the existing unused wells after proper wells.

(*b*) *Crops Irrigated.*

In 1970-71 a total of thirty-six thousand hectares were under all irrigated crops. Food crops accounted for as much as thirty-three thousand hectares. The important irrigated food crops were

TABLE 3.10: **Number of Energised Wells**

(*Numbers*)

Years	*Energised Wells*
1980-81	11430
1881-82	11933
1982-83	12941
1983-84	14370

Source: Board of Revenue (Land Records), Rajasthan, Ajmer.

wheat, barley gram and pulses. The irrigated area under different crops during the last four years ending with 1983-84 is given in Table 3.11.

While going through the Table it is clear that the important irrigated food crop is wheat. After this barley and bajra, etc. wheat constituted a good percentage among all crops in this district during the last four years. To sum up, wheat and barley among cereals and pulses gram among pulses were the crops which received substantial benefit of irrigational facilities. The fall in the irrigated area under the maize is rather alarming, steps should be taken up to stop the fall in the irrigated acreage of cereals and fodder crops because both these are vitally needed for the well being of human and cattle population of this district.

5. Conclusion

(*i*) *Possibilities of Readjustment and Future Development*

The foregoing discussion in this chapter reveals that the production of major crops has recorded a substantial increase. This is a happy sign in the context of the food problem of the country. However, it is a well known fact that the cultivation of non-food crops bring better returns to the farmers and from this point of view results the fall in hectares production and average production (per hectare) of cash crops like cotton and pulses does not augur well. The cash crop occupied less than 5 per

TABLE 3.11: **Irrigated Area Under Different Important Crops in The District**

(Hectares)

Year	*Bajra*	*Percent-age to total irrigated area*	*Wheat*	*Percent-age to total irrigated area*	*Barley*	*Percent-age to total irrigated area*	*Maize*	*Percent-age to total irrigated area*	*Total net Irriga ted area*
1980-81	1329	2.5	17953	34.5	15158	29.1	37	0.07	52080
1981-82	1318	2.3	22656	39.6	17908	31.3	10	0.01	57268
1982-83	3416	4.8	29767	42.5	17632	25.2	25	0.03	70025
1983-84	26808	4.9	34228	31.7	16495	15.3	236	0.22	107849

Source : Statistical Abstract, Rajasthan Volume For Various Years, 1980 to 1984.

cent of the total cropped area. If this trend continues apart from the diminishing the cash returns of the cultivator. It may also adversely affect the fertility of the soil.

What is needed is the balanced agricultural policy in which food crops and fodder crops, both may occupy their proper place to provide a scientific rotation of crops and a firm base to the cash economy of the agriculturist. A continuous fall in food crops will adversely affect the growth of industries as well.[6]

Our enquiries and group discussion with rural folks and with the experts in the field of agricultural technology brought us to the conclusion that no large scale readjustment in the present cropping is possible without a simultaneous expansion in the irrigation facilities. The texture of soil and the climatic conditions place their limitations. However, in this connection we feel that there is a great necessity of shifting some area from the raising of cereals to fruits and vegetables cultivation. As has been said in the chapter on income, expenditure and consumption pattern. The diet of rural population is highly deficient in nutrition which can be made up substantially if the consumption of cheap fruits like banana, papaya and fresh vegetable is increased. This will provide a more balanced diet to the people of this district.

One great advantage with these crops is that there can be sown in rotation crops with cereals and can also be cultivated in sub marginal and newly reclaimed lands. Such subsidiary foods will on the one hand be highly increasing in yield and on the other, be able to support (compared with cereals) a much large number of people per hectare of land. The State Government should launch an extensive programme for the production of major crops, consumption of more fruits, vegetable and provide the necessary facilities.

(*ii*) *Changing in Cropping Pattern*

Looking to the figures of the crop area for the last 10 years, one feels that there has not been any significant shift from one crop to another. Also no near crops on any appreciable scale

6. Agriculture Price Policy, Facts and Issues Involved, *Agriculture Banker* (No. 1, VI, No. 2, 1981).

have been introduced. This may have been due to the fact that the district so far has had no assured means of irrigation. However, there has been a definite shift in preference for hybrid seeds from the conventional seeds.

The present irrigation facilities in this district are rather insufficient and progress during the last four years has been slow. There is no doubt that the yield of crops can increase considerably if proper irrigation facilities are made available. Efforts should be made to construct new wells in large numbers and deepen the existing wells. It has many advantages also over the other sources of irrigation. In actual practice, the cropping pattern is better in areas irrigated by wells and the average yields are higher.

One serious problem with well irrigation is the shortage of power for lifting water. At present bullocks are used for draining water but the capacity of a pair of bullocks is inadequate to utilise the water of a well fully.[7] The use of pumping sets could be popularised by block development authorities or panchayats.

In order to have properly irrigated crops, the optimum quantity of water should be applied to the crops. For this, it is necessary to know the water requirements of each crop. There is a mistaken belief among cultivators that the larger the quantity of water applied to the crops, the better is the yield. But too much watering harms the plants.

Efforts should also be made to conserve rain water by construction of small tanks in areas wherever possible; such tanks will not only provide water for irrigation of the Rabi crop but will also raise the water level of the wells in the vicinity. The beds of these tanks can be utilised for growing crops after they get dry.

7. B.D. Dhanwa, Development of Tubewell Irrigation in India, *Land Bank Journal, Minor Irrigation Special Number*, (December 1979, AGRICO New Delhi, 1982.

4

Rural Indebtedness and Rural Finance

Rural indebtedness and rural finance are co-related financing problems. While the former tells the story relating to the problems of loans that have already been entrusted to the rural people, the latter makes one aware of the problems connected with financing to rural people. Rural credit becomes a problem when it is available adequately in a desired form and supports the farmer in building his assets. The cultivator uses this money which he has received on easy terms to pay off his other debts and get himself relieved of some of his fiscal burdens.

Because of the agrarian base, the earnings of all the households are dependent upon rainfall. Its capricious nature leads many households to incur debts for meeting their day to day requirements; heavy debts have also to be incurred for meeting social obligations, etc.[1] Most of debts are utilised for unproductive purposes and investment in agricultural sector occupies a second place. The problem of rural finance has become very acute. The pressure of population on land is continuously increasing and per capita income of a major portion of population is going down.

The rural indebtedness has been presented under two heads:

(i) Agricultural Sector
(ii) Non-Agricultural Sector

---

1. Report of the Committee to Review Arrangements for Institutional Credit for Agriculture and Rural Development, Bombay, Reserve Bank of India, 1981.

1. Agricultural Sector

Rural indebtedness has been marked incredibly much in the agricultural sector. A sample survey of 1427 agricultural persons was made and it was surprisingly found that 57.25 per cent of people were in debt. The outstanding loan in the agricultural sector forms 85.37 per cent of the total outstanding loans in the rural area of the Sikar district in the year ending 1983-84.

2. Non-Agricultural Sector

Of the total sample population of 260 persons in the non-agricultural sector, 55.38 per cent of the non-agricultural population is indebted. Out of 54 households in the non-agricultural sector, 51.85 per cent of the households are indebted. The outstanding loan in the non-agricultural sector constitutes 14.63 per cent of the total outstanding loan in the rural sector of the Sikar district in the year ending 1983-84. A clear picture of the rural indebtedness has been presented in Table 4.1.

It is evident from the Table that more than 50 per cent of the rural population in both agricultural and non-agricultural sectors is indebted. The size and extent of indebtedness is greater in the agricultural sector.

It is evident from Table 4.2 that more than 50 per cent of the indebted non-agricultural population is in the lowest loan group of Rs 0-100 with per household loan of Rs 33 and per capita loan of Rs 11. Taking the entire rural population, 3.47 per cent of indebted households with 2.60 per cent of indebted persons are in the lowest loan group of Rs 0-100 with an average household loan of Rs 55 and per capita loan of Rs 13.20. 34.68 per cent of the indebted household are in the next higher loan group of Rs 100-300 with an average household loan of Rs 181.70 and per capita loan of Rs 37.33. 44.51 per cent of indebted household are in the loan group of Rs 300-1000 with an average household loan of Rs 472.14 and per capita loan of 83.19. 79.19 per cent of indebted household covering 75.86 of indebted persons are in the loan group of Rs 100-1000 with per capita loan of Rs 64.82 and per household loan of Rs 344.94.

TABLE 4.1: **Rural Indebtedness During the Year 1983-84**

S. No.	*Items*	*Agricultural Sector*	*Non-Agricultural Sector*	*Total*
1.	Sample population	1427	260	1687
2.	Number of indebted persons in sample population.	817	144	961
3.	Percentage of indebted persons.	57.25	55.38	56.96
4.	Sample household	265	54	319
5.	Number of indebted household in sample	145	28	173
6.	Percentage of indebted household	54.72	51.85	54.23
7.	Outstanding loan in Rs	82626	14160	96786
8.	Percentage of the total loan	85.37	14.63	100
9.	Per capita loan*	101.13	98.33	100.71
10.	Per household loan**	569.83	505.71	559.46

*Calculated with reference to indicated persons only.
**Calculated with reference to indicated household only.

Source: Office of the Assistant Registrar of Co-operatives, Societies, Sikar.

3. Sources of Loans

On the distribution of the total outstanding loans in the agricultural sector among the sources from which they were derived,[2] it was found that the co-operative societies or other government agencies did not make any advance in this sector.

2. Financing of Agriculture by Commercial Banks, Report of a Sminar, held on December 6 to 8, 1978, Bombay, Reserve Bank of India 1979.

TABLE 4.2: **Burden of Debt According to Size of Loan Durinng the Year Ending 1983-84**

Agricultural Sector

Size of Loan	Population indebted (sample)	Percentage of total indebted persons (sample)	Household indebted (sample)	Percentage of total indebted household (sample)	Outstanding Loan in sample household	Loan per Household	Loan per Capita
1	*2*	*3*	*4*	*5*	6	*7*	*8*
0-100	23	2.81	5	3.45	297	59.40	12.91
100-300	239	29.25	49	33.79	9209	187.94	38.53
300-1000	377	46.15	66	45.52	31488	477.09	83.52
1000-2000	125	15.30	18	12.41	22716	1262.00	181.73
2000 & above	53	6.49	7	4.83	18916	2702.28	356.90
Tolal :	817	100.00	145	100.00	82626	569.83	101.73

Non-Agricultural Sector

0-100	3	2.08	1	3.57	33	33.00	11.00
100-300	53	36.81	11	39.29	1693	153.90	31.94
300-1000	60	41.67	11	39.29	4867	442.45	81.11
1000-2000	16	11.11	3	10.71	3534	1178.00	220.87
2000 & above	12	8.33	2	7.14	4033	2016,50	336.08
Total :	144	100.00	28	100.00	14160	505.71	98.33

Total Rural Sector

0-100	25	2.60	6	3.47	330	55.00	13.20
100-300	292	30.39	60	34.68	10902	181.70	37,33
300-1000	7	45.47	77	44.51	36355	472.14	83.19
1000-2000	142	14.78	21	12.14	26250	1250.00	184.85
2000 & above	65	6.76	9	5.20	22949	2549.89	353.04
Total :	531	100.00	173	100.00	96786	559.45	100.71

Source: Office of the Assistant Registrar of Co-cperative Sccieties, Sikar (1983-84).

They turned to moneylenders for assistance. A sample survey reveals that in the agricultural sector, 129 out of 145 sample households received loans from moneylenders, 5 households from co-operative societies, 3 households from the government, 3 households from relatives and friends, 5 households from more than one source. Only 5.52 per cent of the indebted agricultural households, and 6.49 per cent of the indebted agricultural population received financial assistance from co-operative agencies and the government. 88.96 per cent of indebted households borrowed from moneylenders during the year ending 1983-84.

A sample survey revealed that out of 28 indebted household in non-agricultural sector, 26 turned to moneylenders for assistance and 2 borrowed the amount from relatives. In terms of percentage 92.86 per cent of indebted non-agricultural household borrowed from moneylenders and 7.14 per cent from other sources, like relatives and friends, etc. The source-wise distribution has been presented in Tables 4.3 and 4.4.

TABLE 4.3: **Source-Wise Distribution of Loan During the Year Ending 1983-84**

(*Agriculture Sector*)

S. No.	*Source*	*Sample household*	*Percentage to total sample*	*Population sample*	*Percentage to total sample*
1.	Moneylender	129	88.96	714	87.39
2.	Co-operative	5	3.45	37	4.53
3.	Government	3	2.07	16	1.96
4.	Others (Friends and Relations)	3	2.07	23	2.82
5.	More than one source	5	3.45	27	3.30
	Total	145	100.00	817	100.00

Source: Office of the Assistant Registrar of Cooperative Societies, Sikar.

TABLE 4.4: **Source-Wise Distribution of Loan During the Year Ending 1983-84**

(Non-agriculture sector)

S. No.	*Source*	*Sample household*	*Percentage to sample household*	*Sample population*	*Percent age to sample population*
1.	Moneylender	26	92.86	136	94.44
2.	Co-operative	—	—	—	—
3.	Government	—	—	—	—
4.	Others (Friends and Relatives)	2	7.14	8	5.56
5.	More than one source	—	—	—	—
	Total	28	100.00	144	100.00

Source: Office of the Assistant Registrar, Cooperative Societies, Sikar.

4. The Purpose of Loan

Any study of rural indebtedness will be incomplete without a study of the purposes for which loans are taken. For this point of view, loans may be classified broadly under three heads: (a) Productive (b) Non-Productive, and (c) Domestic.

A productive loan may be defined as a loan which is to be used to increase the income of the borrower. A non-productive loan is primarily used for consumption purposes in connection with social and religious ceremonies including marriage and death feast which are so common all over the country.[3] A

3. It should be remembered that the entire expenditure incurred in connection with social and other ceremonies cannot be regarded as avoidable. In society the customary rules have more or less the force of law on a person. To that extent, expenses on feast and marriage or at death become obligatory. However, if the expenditure is controlled in a proper way some of the unnecessary expenses can be avoided.

TABLE 4.5: Distribution of Loan in Agriculture Sector According to the Purpose During the Year Ending 1983-84

S. No.	*Purpose*	*Sample agricul- ture household*	*Percentage to sample*	*Sample agricul- ture popula- tion*	*Percent- age to sample*	*Outstan- ding loan in sample agriculture household*	*Percen- tage to sample*
1.	Unproductive loan for social and other ceremonies (avoidable)	37	25.52	211	25.83	28268	34.20
2.	Unproductive loan for domestic consumption and other purposes (unavoidable)	84	57.93	477	58.38	38671	46.80
3.	Productive loan for Agriculture and business	17	11.72	92	11.26	9473	11.47
4.	For more than one purpose.	7	4.83	37	4.53	6214	7.53
	Total ..	145	100.00	817	100.00	82626	100.00

Source: Office of the Assistant Registrar of Cooperative Societies, Sikar.

domestic loan is the unproductive loan due to the fact that a domestic loan is the unavoidable and is used to meet primary needs of the family when the income falls short of the minimum amount necessary to meet the bare necessities of life. An unproductive loan is an indication of extravagance of the borrower. But the domestic loan is not so. Thus, for the purpose of this study loans have been classified. The distribution of loan has been presented in Table 4.5.

It is clear from Table 4.5 that distribution of loan for different purposes in the agriculture sector is different from that of the non-agriculture sector. Whereas 46.80 per cent of the total outstanding loan in the agricultural sector was spent on demestic consumption and allied purposes, the non-agricultural sector availed itself of 64.54 per cent (55.86+8.68) of the total loan for the same purpose. 34.20 per cent of the total loan in agricultural sector was spent on social ceremonies as compared to 23.52 per cent in the non-agricultural sector. However, the expenditure for productive purposes was 11.47 per cent in the non-agricultural sector.

It is evident from Table 4.6 that the total outstanding loans in this sector were for domestic consumption purposes as against 67.86 per cent of indebted non-agricultural households which borrowed 55.86 per cent of the outstanding loans in the non-agricultural sector for domestic consumption. This shows that the economic condition of an average household in the agricultural sector is somewhat better than the economic condition of an average household in the other.

5. Pressure on Land as Causes of Indebtedness (Rural)

Because of heavy pressure on land, the per capita income of a major portion of population is low. People are not able to earn enough to meet the expenditure. The pressure on land of indebted families has been presented in Table 4.7.

It is evident from the Table 4.7 that a major portion of indebted agricultural households (83.26 per cent) is connected in two low land possessed group, and their family budget is a deficit budget. Of the remaining 16.74 per cent indebted families or 14.24 per cent of the total population earns a little above the margin of their expenditure. Only 4.03 families are 4.62 percent of the total population earn much more

TABLE 4.6: **Distribution of Loan in Non-Agricultural Sector According to the Purpose During the Year Ending 1983-84**

S. No.	*Purpose*	*House-hold sample*	*Percen-tage to sample*	*Sample popul-ation*	*Percen-tage to sample*	*Outsta-nding loan*	*Percent-age*
1.	Domestic consumption	19	67.86	90	62.50	7910	55.86
2.	Social ceremonies	7	25.00	39	27.08	3330	23.52
3.	Productive loan for agricultural business	1	3.75	9	6.25	1690	11.94
4.	For more than one purpose	1	3.75	6	4.17	1230	8.68
	Total	28	100.00	144	100.00	1416	100.00

Source: Office of the Asstt. Registrar of Cooperative Societies, Sikar.

TABLE 4.7: **Pressure on Land of Indebted Families During the Year Ending 1983-84**

(Agricultural Sector Hectares %)

Land	*Percentage of indebted household*	*Percentage of indebted population*	*Average size of landholding possessed*	*Average size of landholding cultivated*	*Average size of family member*	*Population pressure on an hectare cultivated land*	*Per capita income*	*Per capita expenditure*	*Savings or Deficit*
0— 5	57.85	52.91	2.66	2.05	5.06	2.47	10.15	12.52	—
5— 10	25.41	28.23	6.71	4.17	6.14	1.47	13.67	14.46	—
10— 15	10.98	12.06	11.28	6.25	6.91	1.06	14.93	13.50	+
15— 20	2.88	3.09	16.13	8.31	5.93	0.71	21.16	15.61	+
20— 25	1.73	2.18	21.31	11.93	7.88	0.66	17.32	17.08	+
25 & above	1.15	1.53	65.65	37.86	8.80	0.23	24.69	20.98	+
Total	100.00	100.00	5.35	3.39	5.37	1.34	12.46	13.35	—

Source: Office of the Assistant Registrar of Cooperative Societies, Sikar.

that what they spend. The average size of holding possessed and cultivated per family in this group is 6.71 and 4.67 hectares respectively against the average size of the family of 6.14 membears. 1.47 members thus, depend upon every cultivated hactare of land, per capita income in this land possessed group works out to be Rs 13.67 and the expenditure per capita comes to Rs 14.46.

So far indebtedness of population in the non-agricultural sector is concerned, it is found that 47.79 per cent of the indebtedness families or 53.24 per cent of the total indebted population derive their income from more than one occupation and yet they earn less than what they are to spend. The monthly per capita income is Rs 10.70 and expenditure Rs 13.98. The remaining population earns a little more above the margin of their expenditure, These facts have been presented in Table 4.8.

TABLE 4.8: **Pressure on Land of Indebted Families During the Year Ending 1983-84**

(Non-Agricultural Sector)

S. No.	*Occupation*	*Percentage of total indebted house*	*Percentage of total indebted population*	*Per capita consumption expenditure*	*Per capita income*	*Savings or Deficit*
1.	Single occupation	52.21	46.75	13.68	14.30	+
2.	More than one	47.79	53.25	13.98	10.70	—
3	All	100.00	100.00	13.73	12.50	—

Source: Office of the Assistant Registrar of Cooperative Societies, Sikar.

While going through Table 4.8, it is clear that in case of non-agricultural indebted population, only 53.25 per cent of the indebted population has a dificit budget as compared to 81.14 per cent in the agricultural sector.

6. Causes of Rural Indebtedness

Various studies have indentified the main reasons for the presence and growth of rural indebtedness.[4] Careful enquirers have been revealed that the main cause of the debt today is the debt of yesterday and the chief obstacle in the way of relief is the indifferent attitude of the poorer classes towards this customary feature of their life as they are born poor, poorly they live and they die in the same fashion. Some of the main causes responsible for rural indebtedness can be categorised as under :

(*i*) *The Ancestral Debt*

The most important and chief cause of the existing indebtedness is the ancestral debt, which prolongs over and persists in from father to son, generation after generation without any equitable restrictions. Children born in debt are found making every possible effort to pay back the debt of their father and forefathers. They are ignorant of the law that the debt of the deceased passes on to the hier only to the extent of property inherited by the latter and if no property is inherited there remains no liability to pay off the debt. They borrow money from one moneylender to pay off another and this practice goes on to increase the debt. Under religious and social obligations, the burden of debt goes on increasing and this become hereditary in a way.

(*ii*) *Illiteracy*

Private moneylenders live in the locality of borrowers. They know sources of their income. Causes of their pressing needs and try to save face value of borrowers at the time of disputes and other risks. The majority of farmers are illiterates, have a weak decision-making power and are incapable of making good plans for themselves or having knowledge to judge the intention of moneylenders in money lending business.

(*iii*) *Vagaries of the Climatic Condition and Other Calamities*

India is subjected to frequent failure of rains and the resultant famines. The frequency of failure of crops due to drought

4. Review Committee Report for Institutional Credit for Agriculture and Rural Development, 1979, Reserve Bank of India.

or flood, hailstorms, insects, beasts and diseases causes the farmer to go to moneylenders who in turn exploit him according to his will. Farmers borrow for almost every thing, i.e. for seeds, cattle, clothing, and even for their food. These situations put them in debt.

(*iv*) *Litigation*

The litigation is realy unfortunate for the Indian farmers which adds to their poverty and unproductive debt. Many persons are required to visit courts either as a party or as a witness throughout the year and waste in this process a lot of money which makes the debt heavy on them.

(*v*) *Liberal Financing*

Adequacy of loan is also a factor for increasing the indebtedness. Those who get protection from high-ups, do not repay their loans or they do delay in repayment. Strictness in recovery has been found a vital point to raise up the extent of recovery. Liberal finance has made the borrowers courageous to borrow. The increase in the extent recovery of co-operative credit is always found due to the use of coercive force. The decision of liberal financing is an important reason for increase in the extent of debt.

(*vi*) *High Rate of Interest*

The high rate of interest also compels the rural people to borrow. The continuous growth in rates of interest and the total principal amount compels the borrower to borrow from other sources to pay the annual interest either to reduce the total payable amount or accept the increased amount as burden of debt. Sometimes the loan goes on accumulating on compound interest and becomes more than the principal.

(*vii*) *Willfulness of Borrowers for Non-payment of Loans* to financiers due to certain reasons is also a cause for indebtedness.

(*viii*) *Lack of Adequate Marketing Facilities is* another factor. The farmers have to sell their produce at a cheaper rate which causes economic hardship at the family level.

With the effect of indebtendness the farmer, who wanted to

increase his income, has to transfer his land or divide it and even to sell it out at cheaper rates. Thereby bringing about economic degeneration in rural society. The farmers, sometimes are compelled to sell their produce at non-profitable rates to the moneylenders. With the lack of savings in the reinvestment plan does not operate. Lack of funds and depressed mentality of the farmer lead to lesser productivity of his land.

7. Debt Relief And Rural Finance

The planners, economists and the governmental bodies think that the rural economic developmet is the crying need of the hour in a country like India. But the mounting increase in the rural indebtendness puts a drag on the economy and causes hinderance to rural development.[5] At times, government suggested various corrective measures to overcome these problems. The following steps are presented to provide debt relief to the rural people:

(a) To Remove the Need for Borrowing

Agriculture has now become a commercial venture and to meet the credit requirements for the use of fertilizers, hybrid seeds, pesticides and insectisides, etc. the farmers have to approach various credit institutions. With a view to provide an infrastructure for cultivation the government has taken various steps to check the increasing trend of rural debt. Some of the important steps suggested for this purpose are mentioned here:

(i) to reduce the heavy burden of land revenue, and make its payments convenient through greater efficiency into administration and collection;
(ii) to increase facilities of irrigation so that dependence of the vagaries of monsoon are reduced;
(iii) to make available the essential agricultural inputs, viz. seeds, fertilizers, insecticides, pesticides, etc. at cheap

5. Lead Bank Scheme, District Credit Plan—New Guidelines, Role of Reserve Bank of India in the sphere of Rural Credit, RBI, 1980.

rates, suitable steps have also to be taken to improve the quality of these inputs;

(iv) to develop allied activities to agriculture like dairy, poultry, piggery, sericulture and bee keeping, etc.;

(v) to promote village and cottage industries, etc.;

(vi) to improve means of communication and transportation and marketing facilities, so as to enable the cultivator to obtain remunerative price for his produce;

(vii) to consolidate the land; and

(viii) to protect the assets of agriculturists from passing into the hands of moneylenders.

This committee reported that the moneylenders evaded the provisions of the moneylenders' Act and thus a pronote was obtained for a larger amount than what was advanced by way of principal; camputing of interest at very high rate than what was stipulated under the Acts. Making of a separate pronote for obtaining extra interest in the name of a future safety, undertaking conditional sale and forward purchases and false evaluation of the doctor's produce taking over of the debtors land of usefructuary mortgage on terms which implied the charging of illegal interest. Thus the powerful moneylenders somehow or the other evaded all the important provisions of these Acts. As a result, very limited success could be achieved in the matter of debt relief.

8. Rural Finance

It is essential to assess the quantum of resources likely to be available in the District for successful implementation of the District Credit plan—1983-1985:

The financial institutions which are working in the district and are primarily responsible to provide necessary credit for the plan are (i) commercial banks, (ii) regional rural banks, (iii) central cooperative bank, (iv) primary land development bank, (v) Rajasthan Finance Corporation, now NABARD, will provide refinance to commercial banks for certain projects sanctioned by them.

One of the most important sources of resource availability is accretion of deposits. Table 4.9 gives position of deposits of commercial banks and regional rural banks for the last four years.

TABLE 4.9: Accretion of Deposits During the Year Ending 1983-84

(*Amount in lakhs*)

Years	*Deposits*	*Percentage increase over previous year*
1980—81	12.75	52.7
1981—82	16.75	31.4
1982—83	23.75	41.8
1983—84	30.45	28.2

Source: Annual Action Plan 1984, District Sikar.

TABLE 4.10: Credit Structure

(*Rs in lakhs*)

Year	*Loan Distributed SF/MF/AL/RA, etc. by Cooperative Banks*	*Loan Distributed SF/MF/AL/RA, etc. by Commercial Banks*
1980—81	37.33	59.53
1981—82	30.72	53.31
1982—83	50.46	60.67
1983—84	41.55	65.67
Annual capacity of loan distributed by Cooperative Banks	385.03	—
Commercial Banks	—	502.30
Branches of 3 Co-operative banks	1.11	80

Source: District Rural Development Agency, Sikar.

TABLE 4.11: **Resource Availability for Loaning Programme During the Year Ending 1983-84**

S.No.	*Institutions*	*Deposits*	*Recoveries (out of earlier loans)*	*NABARD Refinance*	*IDBI Refinance*
1.	Panjab National Bank (Lead Bank)	125000	5800	4789	162
2.	State Bank of India	11500	462	109	72
3.	State Bank of Bikaner & Jaipur	140000	3000	1250	900
4.	Bank of Baroda	75000	1500	351	468
5.	Central Bank of India	9000	250	200	90
6.	Dena Bank	8000	137	100	135
7.	United Commercial Bank	21000	140	106	108
8.	The Bank of Rajasthan Ltd.	13000	200	90	198
9.	The Shekhawati Gramin Bank Ltd.	47000	8411	5562	600

10.	District Central Cooperative Bank Ltd.	22000	45000	4300	—
11.	Sikar Urban Industrial Cooperative Bank Ltd.	3300	4900	—	—
12.	Primary Land Development Bank Ltd.	—	3300	2850	—
13.	Rajasthan Finance Corporation Ltd.	—	3000	—	1278

Source: Annual Action Plan 1984 District Sikar, District Rural Development Agencies, Sikar.

Table 4.9 does not give a clear and constant rate of growth of deposits and reveals fluctuations. It may be due to cycle of drought and good rains, but it may not be termed as only one factor. Th e increase may be attributed to two factors (a) branch expansion by RRB and commercial banks, (b) inward remittance from middle east countries.

Other important source of resource availability is recycling of fund. In this district, over all recovery position of commercial banks including RRB is rather poor.

It is clear from the Table 4.10 that loans distributed by cooperative and commercial banks have been increased year after year due to the expansion of branches at the district level. Table 4.11 clearly shows that the annual capacity of loan distributed by commercial banks is more than that distributed by cooperative banks.

Refinance from NABARD (ARDC) and IDBI have been calculated on the basis of on-going schemes. Thus loanable funds with the commercial banks will be available to fulfil their commitments under the District credit plan 1983-1986. Bank-wise estimates are given in Table 4.11.

5

Rural Industrialisation

Fifty years ago Mahatma Gandhi said that India lives in villages. This statement is true even today as eighty per cent of our country's population lives in rural areas and is dependent on it for its employment and livelihood.[1] Agriculture still continues to be the main occupation of people living in rural areas.

Sikar district has not been known for any important industry. Khandela (a village in the district) however, has been famous for Gota products since long. This industry has been in the cottage industry sector. Other cottage crafts which have been regarded as specialities of this area are wooden toys and tie & dye printing. All these still continue to flourish in the district.

Agriculture is the main occupation of rural people but it cannot be expected to provide employment to the over growing population. The total land which can be brought under the plough is limited whereas population continues to increase at a fast pace. As a result, the pressure of population on land has been increasing. As the holding of land of majority of rural families in this district is small which cannot provide full employment or sufficient income to them. The shift of population in search of work to another places, then is quite obvious.

1. Extent of Disguised Unemployment in the Agricultural Sector

Of a rural population of 1098309 persons, 784632 persons

---

1. Government of India, Evaluation Study of Rural Industries Project, 1978.

or 71.44 per cent of the total population depend on agriculture as their main source of income. 30.27 per cent of the agricultural population consists of male earners and earning dependents in the working age group of 15-55 years.

The question that rises here is whether one can successfully cultivate 7.2 acres of land. The answer does not come in the affirmative only during the sowing and harvesting seasons which approximately extend over 100 days in this district. It will be necessary to have the assistance of one or more adult male persons. For the remaining 265 days in this district (approximately 9 months) the farmer works with the help of his minor non-earning dependents. Of course, for the remaining nine months they are available for employment in sectors other than agriculture. The agricultural sector provides employment for about three months only in a year. The services of the persons for the agricultural sector cannot be shifted because their services are needed during harvesting and sowing as well. So, we have to find gainful employment for these people for at least about 9 months. While considering the ways and means of providing employment to the under-employed, it will be useful to make a study of the existing cottage and village industries and examine their employment potential and present problems.

2. Types of Industries

Rural industries are usually those industries which are engaged in manufacturing, processing, preservation and servicing in villages and small towns utilising locally available natural resources and human skills and small amounts of capital. The various rural industries, can be broadly classified into three categories, viz. (i) Cottage industries, (ii) Agro-based industries, and (iii) Small scale industries.

(*a*) *Cottage Industries*

The important crafts of the area are Gota, Tie & Dye printing, Desi Juti and Wooden toys, etc. Their description in brief is as follows[2] :

2. Office of the District Industries Officer, Sikar and Director, Small Scale Industries Service Institute, Jaipur.

(*i*) *Gota*: This industry is mainly concentrated at Khandela village and can easily be regarded as one of the most important cottage industries of the district. There are about 400 units engaged in Gota production. The main products are Gota-kinari, Lampi, Phool, Bijia, Champa, Naksi, Thappa and Kor, etc. All these items are used in manufacture of ladies garments. The industry provides full-time employment to about 1000 workers and part-time to about 8000 workes (mostly women) of Khandela and adjoining villages. It has been estimated that the total investment in all the units is about Rs 98 lakhs. About a half of the production is sold in Rajasthan and the rest is sold in Haryana, Punjab and Delhi.

(*ii*) *Tie & Dye*: This industry is located at Sikar and Fatehpur. Tie & Dye is a process of cloth printing and the garments on which such printing is done in the district. The items for Tie & Dye are sarees, chunris, peela, pomcha and orhnis. About 50 per cent of the production is sold within the State and the rest goes to States like Assam, Bengal and Bihar.

(*iii*) *Desi Jutis*: About 300 families mostly from the Scheduled Castes (Raigars) earn a livelihood through the manufacture of indigenous shoes. The leather required for the purpose is locally tanned and dyed. The places known for this work are Nechhwa, Gothra and Sikar. The productivity of artisans is at present low due to obsolete tools and techniques used. Demand of Desi Juti is expected to increase due to the growth in population.

(*iv*) *Wool Spinning*: It is an important cottage craft of the area as district occupies an important place in the wool production in the State. The industry provides full and part-time employment to about 38 and 76 workers respectively.

(*v*) *Wooden Toys*: A small number of persons at Khandela are in this profession. This industry provides only part-time employment opportunities.

(*vi*) *Charas*: 'Charas' is a large size leather bucket used for drawing out water from well for irrigation and drinking. On the basis of information available, it has been estimated that about 20 per cent of the hides tanned are used for 'charas' making. A charas can be stitched in two days and leaves roughly Rs 24 to Rs 32 as wages to workers. The demand of charas is closely related to the number of wells. Mostly the use of charas is more during Rabi. Assuming that about 50 per cent of the wells are in full use and remaining are used partly, the demand for charas will certainly go down because of the expansion of electrified wells are going in number day by day.

(*vii*) *Blacksmithy*: In almost every big village, there is a Lohar. In addition to repairing work, he makes articles like an axe, sickles, khurpies, gandasi, knives and pans, etc. Blacksmithy is a basic industry which supplies the tools and implements for other cottage industries. From the point of view of usefulness of the cultivators, blacksmithy is stands first amongst the cottage industries. The blacksmith is paid his wages either in cash or kind. Mostly in villages, about 40 to 50 kg. of grain per family per year is given to blacksmith. But if some special work is to be done, he is paid separately in cash. A blacksmith earns between Rs 150 and Rs 400 per month. More training-cum-production centres should be started at different places in the district. The tarining should mainly be given in manufacturing sectors. The quality of implements produced locally is rather poor, and hence the agriculturists prefer to purchase them from some other cities like Jaipur.

(*viii*) *Pottery*: There is hardly a village which does not have its own potter or Kumhar who employs the traditional techniques for producing a large variety of vessels for domestic use. The raw material is clay which is freely available in villages. Potters usually cater to the needs of the agriculturists and are generally paid in kind. They work for nearly eight months in a year. Even during this period they are not fully employed. The potter will have to change the techniques and quality of his products. He should adopt wheels fitted with ball bearings. The All India Khadi and Village Industries Commission has already distributed some such wheels. Training may, therefore, be imparted to potters for production of improved type of vessels.

(*ix*) *Carpentry*: A carpenter is no less important than a blacksmith for the rural population. He makes and repairs plough, the wooden part of agricultural implements. Carpenters are remunerated either in cash or in kind, according to the nature of the work for which they are engaged. The capital investment of a carpenter varies from Rs 1000 to Rs 1600. The carpenter's products are generally poor in finish. It is recommended that training facilities should be made available to them for improved techniques in the field.

(*x*) *Hand Fan and Basket Manufactute*: This industry is carried on by Raigars, Chamars, Sweepers and Khateeks. About 40 to 50 fans per day can be made by a family. The fans are sold for about 40 paisa each. Electric facility is not available in most of the villages of Sikar district. It is yet to reach the poorer sector of the society in the district. So hand fans will continue to have a brisk demand.

The work of basket making is also carried on with the help of members of family. The capital investment varies from Rs 100 to Rs 300 per unit. The raw material for the industry consists of bamboo and palm leaves. The selling price of a basket depends upon its size.

(*xi*) *Oil Ghani*: The work of extracting oil by Ghani is done in almost all large villages of this district by Telees. The investment per unit varies from Rs 1000 to Rs 1800. The efficiency of Ghani-man depends mainly on the regular supply of oilseeds.

(*b*) *Khadi & Village Industries*

The weavers of the district produce pure khadi (i.e. hand spun and hand woven cloth) as well as handloom (i.e. mill spun but hand woven) cloth. Weaving is not only a secondary occupation of some agriculturists but also the sole occupation of many of them. Handloom industry is one of the oldest industries of this district. The clothes produced are Khesla,

TABLE 5·1: **Progress of Cottage and Village Industries During the Period Ending 1983-84**

S. No.	*Industry*	*Production*		*Sales*		*Employment*	
		Quantity	*Value*	*Quantity*	*Value*	*Full*	*Partial*
1.	Blacksmithy	N.A.	0.10	N.A.	00.71	11	11
2.	Bans Bet	N.A.	0.50	N.A.	1.00	13	26
3.	Ghani Oil	N.A.	18.97	N.A.	26.50	486	486
4.	Lime	N.A.	2.56	N.A.	4.03	26	12
5.	Leather	N.A.	N.A.	N.A.	N.A.	N.A.	N.A.
6.	Pottery	N.A.	2.58	N.A.	2.44	62	88

N.A.: Not Available.

Source: Office of the Secretary, Khadi and Village Industries Board, Jaipur.

Bhakla, Baldhi, Loie, Chotia and Reja, etc. Table 5.2 shows the progress of Khadi industries. This industry is carried on by various types of units, viz. independent workers, master weavers, and the cooperative societies The societies sell their cloth either to wholesalers or through their own sale depots or the depots of khadi/handloom board.

It is evident from Table 5.2 that progress of Khadi industries has not been satisfactory. The contribution of khadi industry in Rajasthan is almost negligible as it attributes only 18 per cent. From the value point of view woollen khadi is more important than cotton khadi.

(c) *Small Scale Industries*

There are no large scale industries in the rural areas of the district. According to a survey conducted by small industries service institute, the district had 117 small scale units at the end of the year 1981-82. Important categories of these are as follows:

TABLE 5.2: **Progress of Khadi Industries During the Year Ending 1983-84**

(*Quantity : Lakh sq. metres*)
(*Value : Lakh Rs*)

Year	*Cotton Khadi*		*Woollen Khadi*		*Total Production*	
	Quantity	*Value*	*Quantity*	*Value*	*Quantity*	*Value*
1981—82	N.A.	3.69	N.A.	37.56	N.A.	41.25
1982—83	0.71	6.18	1.44	42.61	2.15	48.79
1983—84	0.73	6.60	N.A.	24.34	0.73	30.49

N.A. : Not Available.
Source: Office of the Secretary, Rajasthan Khadi and Gramodyog Board, Jaipur.

(*i*) *Iron and Steel Fabrication*: The units are spread over a large area. The places where such units are situated are Sikar, Srimadhopur, Danta Ramgarh and Lachhmangarh. The items of manufacture are trunks, buckets, sheet metal products, agricultural implements and household iron products. The market for the industry is within the district. The employment potential was limited to 139 persons and the value of goods produced was Rs 4.30 lakhs in 1983-84.

(*ii*) *Steel Furniture*: This industry is situated at Sikar town because the demand for the products is mainly urban. They manufacture steel almirahs, cash boxes, sofas and trunks, etc.

(*iii*) *Washing Soap*: Of the three washing soap units of the district, two are situated at Sikar and the third one at Khandela. The washing soap manufactured by these units sells at Sikar, Jhunjhunu and Churu, with an investment of Rs 4.00 lakhs and employment potential of 60 persons in 1983-84.

(*iv*) *Oil and Dal Mills*: There are four such units, two each situated at Sikar and Srimadhopur. They make Dal from moong, moth and gram and oil from sesame, mustard and groundnut. The employment being limited to 60 workers in 1981-82.

(*v*) *Lime and Lime Powder and China Clay*: There are nine units situated at Khokra, Neem-ka-Thana, Maonda, Srimadhopur, Lachhmangarh, Kanwal and Reengus. The lime powder is sent to Mysore, Bengal, Bihar, Maharashtra, Haryana, Uttar Pradesh and Delhi. The industry gave employment to 500 persons and had an investment of Rs 20 lakhs in 1981-82. One of the units has a plant for washing and grinding of china clay also. Its products go to Haryana, Delhi, Goa and Gujarat, etc.

(*vi*) *Cement Products*: Two units each at Sikar and Reengus manufacture cement products, like flower pots, cement screens, water pots, structures, etc. Its investment was Rs 1 lakh and 38 persons were employed in 1981-82.

(*vii*) *Rolling Mill*: A Steel Rolling Mill was set up at Sikar in 1968-69. The production of this mill was valued at Rs 30 lakhs in 1981-82 and it provides employment to 35 persons. The products are sold within Rajasthan,

(*viii*) *Wooden Furniture*: Six registered units are engaged in this line of activity in the district. The largest number (three) being at Danta Ramgarh. The products of these units are wooden cots, tables, chairs, doors, windows and window frames, etc. The market for these products is local with an employment to 46, the value of production in 1981-82 was 74.3 thousand.

(*ix*) *Repacking of Chemicals*: There is only one such small scale unit which was set up in 1972. The chemicals it repacks are glycerine, castor oil and soda bicarb. The repacked chemicals are mostly sold within the district.

(*x*) *Woollen Thread and Cloth*: A unit for the manufacture of woollen thread was established at Sikar in 1961. The total investment in the unit was Rs 7,000 and it provided employment to four persons. The production is sold locally.

There was only one registered woollen cloth small scale unit. It produces rough woollen cloth. The total investment was Rs 13,2000 and employment was provided to nine persons.

(*xi*) *Others*: Some other small units are engaged in the production of such items as stone chips, sodium cilicate, artificial teeth, lac bangles, ice, pan masala, hair oil, washers and strips, reflex valves, beam scales, mineral grinding, ayurvedic medicines, polished cotton parn and candles. There is a unit doing general engineering and repair jobs and another doing tyre-retreading.

3. Industrial Cooperatives

At the end of the cooperative year[3] 1981-82 (ending June 30), there were 73 industrial cooperatives in the district, with a total membership of 733. The gross share capital of these societies put together was Rs 82,904 and the working capital Rs 4.29 lakhs. There were also nine weavers societies, seven for handloom cotton and two for khadi cotton. The membership of weavers' societies was 661. There share capital was Rs 28 thousand and working capital Rs 1.65 lakhs. The borrowing of these societies were Rs 1.15 lakhs of which Rs sixty-two thousand were outstanding. More than 50 per cent of the industrial societies were of leather workers whose membership was 865. The next numerically important group is Teli ghani, where the membership was 183, the number of societies being six.

4. Industrial Training

There is an Industrial Training Institute at Sikar.[4] The institute trains people as welders, electricians, fitters, wiremen and turners. In 1981-82 the total capacity in all trades was 144 and the actual strength 117. The total strength of instructors was eleven.

5. State Aid to Industries

The various sources of industrial finance are banks, the Rajasthan Financial Corporation, the State Government and

---

3. Office of the Registrar, Cooperative Societies, Rajasthan, Jaipur.
4. Office of the Director, Technical Education, Rajasthan, Jodhpur.

the Central financial agencies. Rajasthan Financial Corporation advances long term loans under its own rules. The first loan sanctioned by the Corporation in the district was in April 1959. Up to 1983-84, loans amounting to Rs 660,000 have been sanctioned to various units in the district.

The district is amongst the ones which have been officially declared as backward and are eligible for concessional finance from governmental financial institutions. The concession is given in the form of reduced margin, lesser rate of interest, longer period of moratorium, longer repayment period, etc. The institutes also participate in the share capital by underwriting. There is also a 50 per cent reduction in underwriting commission.

6. Role of Rural Industries in the District Economy

The cause of village industries was championed by Mahatma Gandhi and thereafter the development of khadi and village industries became an integral part of our economic plans.[5] Rural industrialisation provides clinical remedies to many socio-economic ills prevalent in the district. Village industries have a capacity to create mere employment opportunities with low investment and shorter gestation period. These industries are generally labour intensive, the capital required per person employed is much smaller than in the case of large scale industry. They are thus ideal for rural areas where capital is scarce while labour is abundant. The features of rural industries and their role in the rural economy of Sikar district is described here :

(*i*) *Employment Potential*

Village industries have a capacity to create more employment opportunities. Ideal manpower in the rural areas can easily be absorbed in employment due to the simple technology involved.

(*ii*) *Short Gestation Period*

Village industries have a relatively shorter gestation period.

5. Sibnath Bhattacharya, *Rural Industrialisation in India: Its Nature and Problems*, B.R. Publishing Corporation, Delhi 1980.

while large scale units take years to set up and then to attain reasonable levels of capacity utilisation these industries can be constructed and brought into operation in a much less time.

(iii) Balanced Regional Development

Village industries being widely dispersed, are capable of remedying the regional disparities in industrial development.

(iv) Low Cost of Employment

The cost of employment in village industries is very low as compared to small scale and large scale industries. While finances to the tune of Rs 1 lakh to Rs 1.5 lakhs are required to provide employment to one person under large scale industry, only 13000 to 15000 rupees are required in case of cottage and village industries.

(v) Utilisation of Local Resources

Village industries often make use of local resources which, otherwise, may go waste. These industries can make the best possible use of the un-utilised and under-utilised local resources.

(vi) Amelioration of the Agricultural Labourers

Rural industries provide part-time and whole-time employment to the agricultural labourer. These industries provide a supplementary source of income to agricultural labourers during the slack seasons and also to the non-viable marginal farmers.

(vii) Augment Production of Consumer Goods

By producing cheap goods needed for mass consumption, scarcity of such goods can be eliminated, thus exerting an anti-inflationary impact.

(viii) Mobilisation of Savings

Savings in the rural areas remain idle in the absence of any producing activity. Rural savings are generally used for consumption purposes. The growth of rural industries offers investment opportunities to people living in these areas.

(ix) Export

The artistic handicrafts earn valuable foreign exchange for the country. Industries connected with gems, jewellery and carpets, etc. have helped to increase country's export.

These industries have much more flexibility in their operations. They can meet the individual tastes and the changing fashion. Spread of electrification has enlarged the scope for development of rural industries. Decentralisation of production is possible by rural industries and they can also provide a check on excessive and premature urbanisation.

7. Problems and Suggestions of Rural Industries

No doubt the involvement of rural industries in ameliorating the condition of the rural people is of great importance.[6] They can play their rightful role if they are run on sound lines. It is, therefore, necessary to identify various problems being faced by these industries.

(i) Non-Availability of Raw Material

One of the major problems faced by village industries is non-availability of raw material and their exorbitant prices. Often rural industries do not get raw material in time. As a result, these industries very often fail to produce goods of good quality and at cheap rates.

(ii) Inadequate and Exploitative Market

Most of the rural industries are forced to restrict their sales to the local markets. In absence of regulated markets they have to sell their goods at relatively a cheaper rate. Besides, the producer wastes his time in marketing, which could have been used for production.

(iii) Shortage of Finance

One of the major requirements of the rural industries, like

6. Sibnath Bhattacharya, *Rural Industrialisation in India: Its Nature and Problems*, B.R. Publishing Corporation, Delhi, 1980.

any other economic activity is credit and it is extremely difficult and expensive for the poor, resourceless artisans to secure adequate capital on reasonable terms for carrying on their traditional activity. In the absence of adequate and timely availability of credit facilities, the production process gets affected adversely, the bankers, find it difficult to understand their business, organise their activities and finance them in a systematic manner. Finance may be made available to independent units by bringing them under the co-operative fold.

(*iv*) *Outmoded and Traditional Technology*

Rural industries still depend on outmoded and traditional technology which leads to poor productivity and poor quality of goods produced. Poor artisans are neither able to buy new equipment, nor do they know much about new methods and techology.

(*v*) *Composition with Large-Scale Industries*

Rural industries cannot withstand the competition thurst upon by the large-scale industries. Large scale industries organised as these are on modern lines, using the latest technology and having access to many facilities, can easily outsell the small producers.

(*vi*) *Problem of Power*

Rural industries are not concentrated at a particular place due to their nature. Shortage of power supply invariably affects the production cycle of small industries adversely. The small enterprises cannot afford to go in for alternatives like installing own thermal units because of heavy costs involved in it. Besides these problems, the rural industries also face the problem of under-utilisation of their capacity.

8. Suggestions

With a view to solving these problems a few valuable suggestions are mentioned here :

1. The Government should open more training-cum-production centres where the youngmen who intend

to set up their own units may come and receive proper training.

2. The industries department of the State Government should provide the techincal know-how and the necessary equipment. Funds for this purpose may be provided by the Khadi and Village Industries Commission, Rajasthan Financial Corporation and commercial and co-operative banks.
3. Co-operative societies may be formed to look after the supply of raw material and sale of the goods produced.
4. For industries which cannot be taken up by all castes but by certain castes only like flaying, glue making, tanning, etc. It is suggested that Government should get model colonies constructed for them. Such colonies would have the necessary facilities for setting up the industries such as pits for tanning and adequate water arrangements for washing.
5. In order to make the industries remunerative, proper arrangements should be made for the sale of goods produced in urban and rural markets.

   To facilitate this, Industrial Cooperative Societies should be established in villages and Government should provide them financial help to enable them to stand on their own legs.
6. Effective steps should be taken to check adulteration of oil by Chairman. The Panchayat/Societies should be encouraged to penalise the defaulters.
7. Supply of power should be regular.
8. Loans should be made available to independent units by bringing them under cooperative fold.
9. Competition with large scale industries should be avoided because these small industries are not capable of this.

9. Findings

The rationale of industries arising in the rural areas has often been questioned by economists on the ground that it will have less propensity for capital formation. India is an under-developed country where 82 per cent of the total

TABLE 5.3: **Potential Survey of the District Conducted in 1983-84**

Industry	Suggested Location
(*A*) *Resource Base*	
1. Porcelain crockery	Neem-ka-Thana
2. Low tension porcelain	Neem-ka-Thana
3. Woollen textile	Sikar
4. Kikar and Babul gark disintegration	Sikar, Neem-ka-Thana
5. Rope and ban making and reed furniture	Srimadhopur, Neem-ka-Thana, Reengus, Sikar, Danta Ramgarh
6, Leather tanning	Padampura (Sikar)
(*B*) *Demand Based*	
7. Cotton hosiery	Sikar, Fatehpur
8. Paper bags	Sikar
9. Readymade garments	Sikar
10. Plastic toys and novelty goods.	Sikar, Fatehpur, Ramgarh, Lachhmangarh, Srimadhopur, and Neem-ka-Thana

population lives in rural areas. Rural industrialisation is the only answer to remove poverty. It is not desirable to establish centralised industries which require large capital resources which are beyond the capacity of people living in villages. The problem of regional imbalances and concentration of economic power cannot be solved by large industries. Hence, rural industrialisation is expected to diversify rural occupations and provide non-farming opportunities to the surplus population. The problem cf unemployment and under-employment will not be solved unless the cottage and village industries play their effective role in the rural economy of the Sikar district.

10. Industrial Potential

As the district does not possess any large scale industry, there is not much scope for the development of ancillary industries. We conducted a potential survey of the district in 1983-84 and identified a number of small scale industries which could be set up in the district on the basis of either resources or demand. Some of the industries that could be set up in the district as indicated by survey are given in Table 5.3.

6

Rural Development Programmes

'India lives in its villages' is as much true today as it was centuries ago. Nearly 80 per cent of the rural people in the country depend on agriculture and allied activities for their livelihood.[1] The main focus of our planners has been to ameliorate the condition of the rural poor and less privileged people of the rural society. The community development movement, Intensive agricultural district programme, Intensive agricultural area programme, Drought prone area programme, etc. were the outcome of this thinking.

One cannot deny the fact that any kind of strategy for rural development and village upliftment is necessarily associated with farm productivity. Productivity can be made possible by optimum utilisation of national resources, adoption of improved farm technology and timely availability of inputs. Various programmes are launched to provide benefits to the rural poor engaged in agricultural activities.

1. Integrated Rural Development Programme (IRDP)

The Integrated Rural Development Programme in its present form was launched in 1978 in 2300 selected blocks all over the country with a provision to add 300 blocks every year.[2] Looking to the usefulness of this programme, it was extended to all the blocks in the country from 2nd October 1980. As a consequence this programme was implemented in

---

1. M.S. Swaminathan, *Science and Integrated Rural Development*, Concept, New Delhi, 1982.
2. Government of India, Ministry of Rural Reconstruction, Manual on Integrated Rural Development, 1980.

all the 236 blocks of the State from 2nd October, 1980.

The guidelines for implementation of this programme were issued in 1978. Since then a number of issues have been included in these guidelines which are clarified in subsequent circulars. A number of policy decisions have also been taken which have brought about substantial modifications in the approach, coverage and contents of the programme. The programme is a synthesis of the strategies which have been tested and found effective during implementation of special programmes like Development agencies, Command area development agencies and Drought prone area programme. The IRDs' main objective is to bring families in the identified target group above the poverty line and to create substantial additional opportunities for employment in the rural areas. In fact, the programme is also to be seen as an instrument for achieving some of the major objectives of the Sixth and Seventh Plans. The target group consists of the poorest amongst the poor in our rural areas—small and marginal farmers, agricultural and non-agricultural labourers, rural artisans and craftsmen, Scheduled Castes and Scheduled Tribes.

This programme has great potential for bringing about improvement in the standard of living of the most needy sections of India's rural population. Under this programme it is proposed to cover nearly 600 families per block every year and 300 families during the Sixth Five Year Plan period (1980-81 to 1984-85) with a systematic subsidy budget of Rs 5.00 lakhs in the first year, Rs. 6.00 lakhs in the second year and Rs 8.00 lakhs per annum in each of the third, fourth and the fifth year.

Under this programme, a subsidy to the extent of 25 per cent is given to small farmers and 33.05 per cent to marginal farmers, agricultural labourers and rural artisans, etc. subject to a maximum ceiling of Rs 3000 in drought prone area programme and Rs 4000 in drought prone area programme. In case of families belonging to the Scheduled Caste the rate of subsidy is 50 per cent and maximum ceiling is fixed at Rs 5000. For Scheduled Castes families also the rate of subsidy is paid out of Scheduled Caste development corporation fund.[3]

3. IRDP Annual Plan, 1982-83, Rajasthan, SSO, Jaipur.

(i) Procedure of Identification

For ascertaining the economic status and income status and income of the selected target groups, a detailed household survey in respect of block selected area envisaged. About 50 per cent of the families are said to be living below the poverty line. On the basis of the household survey, the families can be classified on the basis of their annual income.

Families falling under the lowest income group should be first covered to provide assistance under the IRD programme. It has been decided that a high priority be given to cover Scheduled Castes and Scheduled Tribes under the programme. It has also been decided that where the percentage of these classes in a block is more than 20, they should be covered under various programmes at least to the proportion which they term to the total population in the selected areas. It is equally important to ensure that at least 20 per cent of the subsidy released and 20 per cent of the credit mobilised should go to families belonging to Scheduled Castes and Scheduled Tribes. Every care be taken to see that SC/ST families receive substantial assistance which should be sufficient to raise their income above the poverty line.

For identifying the beneficiaries under the IRD programme, the Antyodaya approach may be adopted. This approach lays emphasis on the need to extend the benefit first to the poorest amongst the poor. Accordingly, effort should be made to select the poorest of the beneficiaries first and formulate economically viable development programmes for them.[4]

(ii) The Beneficiaries : Selection of Beneficiaries Procedure

The identification of IRD families is done on the basis of guidelines of the Government. As per the procedure the selection of beneficiaries under the IRDP is made by Gram Sabha from the list prepared by Gram Sevak Patwari. A family whose income is less than Rs 700 per annum per person is eligible to be identified as IRD beneficiary.

A study reveals that out of 281 beneficiaries 250 beneficiaries

4. Manual of Integrated Rural Development Programme, Published by Ministry of Rural Reconstruction, Government of India, New Delhi.

(that comes to 88.97 per cent) were selected by the Gram Sabha in an open meeting convened for the purpose, while 22 beneficiaries informed that their selection was made by the Gram Sevaks, wheras the remaining 9 beneficiaries told that their selection was made by the Patwari. Thus, we find that 7.83 per cent beneficiaries were identified by the Gram Sevaks while 3.20 per cent were selected by the Patwari.

The above information reveals that the selection procedure laid down by the Government for identification of IRDP families was not followed properly. But in most of the cases the procedure was adhered to. A slight deviation in the selection procedure was observed in 11.03 per cent cases.

It has also been observed that the beneficiaries other than the list were included and some names from the select list excluded. It so happened that even persons of high socio-economic strata were selected and given benefit under the IRD programme in the year 1981-82 in the surveyed villages of Sikar district.

(*iii*) *Socio-Economic Background of the Selected Beneficiaries*

The socio-economic background of a person plays an important role in making him eligible for getting IRD benefits as per the norms 50.89 per cent beneficiaries belonged to Scheduled Castes, 5.34 per cent were widows and 0.71 per cent were physically handicapped. A major share of benefits extended under this poverty eradication programme flowed towards Scheduled Caste communities. Persons belonging to the age group of 35 to 39 constituted the mode group and as many as 67.26 per cent beneficiaries were uneducated. Looking at the profession of these beneficiaries we found that 27.76 per cent were agricultural labourers followed by marginal farmers and small farmers.

Out of the 281 beneficiaries
2 (0.71%) were in the age group of 15 to 20 years
21 (7.47%) were in the age group of 21 to 25 years
34 12.18%) were in the age group of 26 to 30 years
39 (13.88%) were in the age group of 31 to 35 years
44 (15.66%) were in the age group of 36 to 40 years
143 (50.89%) belonged to Scheduled Caste, and
13 (4.63%) belonged to Scheduled Tribe;

while 15 (5.34%) were widows, 2 (0.71%) were physically handicapped, 1 (0.36%) was bonded labourer and 107 (38.08%) were others. The average size of the families consisted of 5 members. Out of the 281 beneficiaries, 189 (67.26%) were illiterate, 41 (14.59%) were able to read and write, 27 (9.61%) were educated and up to primary standard, 19 (6.71%) were educated up to middle standard, 4 (1.42%) were up to secondary standard and only 1 (0.36%) was graduate.

(*iv*) *Occupation-wise Break-up of the Beneficiaries*

Activity-wise profession adopted by these beneficiaries is as under:

TABLE 6.1: **Occupational Break-up of the Beneficiaries Year 1983-84**

S. No.	*Profession*	*Total No.*	*Percentage*
1.	Small farmers	53	18.86
2.	Marginal farmers	58	20.64
3.	Agricultural labourers	78	27.76
4.	Rural artisans	46	16.37
5.	Rural labourers	27	9.61
6.	Others	19	6.76
	Total	281	100.00

Source: Annual Action Plan, D.R.D.A., Sikar, 1983-84.

The occupation-wise break-up of the interviewed beneficiaries of the selected villages is shown in the above Table.

Agriculture is the most important economic activity being pursued in the selected villages. In a way it is the main source of livelihood for the people irrespective whether they possess or do not possess the land. The link between agricultural occupation and other economic activities is inseparable. Hence, it is easily established that the beneficiaries (39.50%) entirely depend on the cultivation which occupies the first position, and beneficiaries which depend on agriculture labour as well as rural craft.

Housing, Land Holdings, Animal and Other Possession

(*i*) *Housing Position*

The majority of 281 beneficiaries, who were interviewed, either had a pucca house, a half-pucca house or both types of houses. Some beneficiaries were in possession of small huts or kuccha houses. Most of these beneficiaries had no separate arrangement to keep their animals. Only 85 beneficiaries had separate 'baras'* where they kept their animals. The total as per information provided by these beneficiaries for their house property was estimated to the tune of Rs 1350.

(*ii*) *Land Holdings*

145 interviewed beneficiaries (51.60%) had no land at all and the remaining 136 (48.40%) had irrigated or unirrigated or both kinds of land holdings. According to the market price, the total cost of their 478.063 acres of land holdings comes to Rs 14,74,250.00 and unirrigated land (68.95%) to Rs 6,84,500.00. 3 beneficiaries were in possession of both irrigated and unirrigated land.

(*iii*) *Animal Possession and Other Property*

It was observed that the beneficiaries were also in possession of animal property and other things. Goat was the most popular amongst them as 120 beneficiaries were in possession of 416 goats. Bicycle turned out to be the next most popular assets as 16 beneficiaries were in possession of one bicycle each and two beneficiaries had two bicycles each.

(*iv*) *Workers*

Here, it would be interesting to examine as to how many workers in the families of selected beneficiaries were engaged in some type of economic activity and what was the status of the family of these persons. There is a myth that more persons are at work in larger families. But the analysis of the family size and persons at work in our sample reveals that the

*a fold for animals.

maximum number of persons was at work in the family size of six. An average family size of IRD beneficiaries is 5.5. In all 281 beneficiaries families were having population of 1557. On an average, 1.44 per cent persons were engaged in work in each family.

(v) The Benefits Provided

All the benefits (to interviewed beneficiaries only) under IRD programme extended in Sikar district during the period under review can be classified into four broad categories:

1. Agriculture
2. Animal husbandry
3. Minor irrigation
4. Teritiary sector including IGB and self wage employment under TRYSEM.

(vi) Training of Rural Youth for Self-employment

164 persons got benefit under animal husbandry. If we add 65 units pertaining to agricultural sector which were allotted to the beneficiaries and comprised bullock pairs, camel carts, buffaloes carts and donky units. The total number of beneficiaries which were provided animals as IRD benefits comes to 229, which is roughly 81.49 per cent of the total beneficiaries. This leads to conclude that animal programme has emerged as a major IRD benefit programme only 18.51 per cent beneficiaries received their benefits not connected with animals. Most of the beneficiaries were engaged in more than one economic activity due to which they have been included in more than one activity. The comparison clearly depicts that during the period 1984-85 as a result of IRD programme benefit agriculture and animal sector got a boost up and more families started entering into these areas.

(vii) Classification of Families

From the point of view of the study, families have been classified into two broad categories, i.e. below the poverty line and above the poverty line.

As is evident from Table 6.2 that 68 beneficiaries were actually benefited who crossed the poverty line during the

TABLE 6.2: **Classification of Families**

S. No.	*Income of Familys*	*No. of Families*	
		1980-81	*1983-84*
1.	Below the poverty line	195	127
2.	Above the poverty line	86	154
	Total	281	281

Note: Here the poverty line means that per person annual income of families is less than Rs 700.

Source: Annual Action Plan, D.R.D.A., Sikar, 1984-85.

period under study. Personal reactions of selected persons reveal that their selection was genuine and they belonged to the economically weaker section of the society. Only one person was hesitant in admitting that he belonged to an economically weaker section. How his name was included in the list of beneficiaries is a matter of further investigation.

(*viii*) *Survey Methodology Purpose*

The purpose of this study is to assess the impact of this programme on economic conditions of persons who live below the poverty line and to evaluate the extent to which they have been benefited.

(*ix*) *Methodology and Design*

In selected villages all the available beneficiaries were approached and interviewed. While selecting the villages, special care was taken to cover all the major viable schemes, activities being executed in the district. In the study 48 villages on a stratified sampling basis were selected for investigation and out of the total 652 beneficiaries only 281 could be contacted as others were not available. While selecting the villages a care was taken to cover all the on-going programmes under the integrated rural development programme in Sikar district.

In addition to the primary data, wherever necessary, the secondary data were also collected to verify the extent to which the programme of IRD has been implemented. The information was also collected by interviewing the Block Development Officer, Pradhans, Bank Managers, Tehsildars and Sarpanchs of concerned areas about various problems being confronted by them implementing the programme.

The primary data were also collected through questionnaires concerning various aspects such as the type of family, literacy background, landholding, housing, caste, occupation, environment, location of the area, public amenities, income expenditure, borrowing,source of borrowing and relations with administration and politicians. The study covered 281 beneficiaries that comes to 6.7 per cent of the total beneficiaries who could be contacted. Out of these 266 were male and 15 female. All the female beneficiaries were widows. A 'sample checking' was carried out in one village in each 'Panchayat Samiti'. Its objective was to ensure the reliability of the information collected.

(*x*) *Role of Financial Institutions & DRDA*

Likewise the dates on which the applications were received and verified by the banks could not be ascertained in the absence of any authentic information. It was observed that the applications which were prepared under IRD beneficiaries scheme were for the total units cost of the benefit unit where as the banks and financing institutions were to sanction the amount (unit cost minus subsidy). The subsidy amount was released to the beneficiaries in most cases whose loans were sanctioned. All the beneficiaries were very much interested and conscious about the subsidy which constituted the total part of the loan sanctioned.

In 48 selected villages 993 applications were received by the banking institutions under the IRD programme during 1983-84 and their total unit cost was Rs 3289285.00. Banking institutions sanctioned loan to 862 applicants (which comes to 86.98 per cent of the total applications) for various purposes. The amount of loan to all these 862 applicants amounted to Rs 1691514.00 excluding subsidy. The subsidy on this sanctioned amount was Rs 118,115.00. Hence, the total benefit extended to these 862 comes to Rs 28,72,666.00. Table 6.3 shows

TABLE 6.3: **Purpose-wise Loan Distribution Year Ending 1983-84**

Items		Applications No. of Units	Prepared Amount in Rs
A.	Agriculture	235	906025
B.	Animal husbandry	602	2044900
C.	Minor irrigation	—	—
D.	Tertiary sector including I.S.B. and Self-wage employment under TRYSEM	—	—

Source : Annual Action Plan (1984-85), DRDA, Sikar.

purpose-wise distribution of the loan applications prepared and amount demanded therein.

The district rural development agency, Sikar after scrutinising 862 sanctioned applications found 767 cases eligible for subsidy.An amount of Rs 10,59,848.00 was sanctioned by DRDA as subsidy against the proposed subsidy outlay of Rs 11,81,152,00. Hence, only 77.24 per cent of the prepared applications were accepted for the release of subsidy by DRDA.

After having received the sanctioned applications of 30 cases the DRDA released subsidy of Rs 40317 within a period of 15 days, in 247 cases if released the subsidy of Rs 3,61,835 within a months period and in 490 cases of released the subsidy of Rs 6,56,6'4 in more than one month.

It is evident from Table 6.4 that actual disbursement was made only to 652 beneficiaries of selected villages. In total 993 applications were prepared out of which 862 were sanctioned by the DRDA for the release of subsidy, whereas only 652 beneficiaries of selected villages were given actual benefit of loan and subsidy.

TABLE 7.4 : **Actual Loan and Subsidy Disbursed to Beneficiaries of 48 Selected Villages Year Ended 1983-84**

S.No.	*Sector*	*Unit No.*	*Loan Rs*	*Subsidy Rs (%)*	*Total Rs*
1.	Agriculture	159	376993	204292 (24.39%)	581287
2.	Animal husbandry	402	749874	509293 (61.66%)	1259167
3.	Minor irrigation	—	—	—	—
4.	Tertiary	91	106990	55370 (13.96%)	162360
	Grand Total :	652	123857	768957	2002814

Source : Annual Action Plan, 1984-85, DRDA, Sikar.

(*ix*) *Integrated Rural Development Review*

(*a*) *Targets*: All the 8 Panchayat Smities, of the district were entrusted with the task of execution of IRD programme in their areas. For these Panchayat Samities 'block plan' of Rs 132.26 lakhs was prepared. It was porposed that with this they would cover 3753 families which were identified as being below the poverty to help these in crossing the proverty line during this period. It was thought that with the help of assistance made available to them, these families would be able to cross the poverty line and also sustain it. They were provided with the meaningful economic activity as provided in the block plan.

A provision of Rs 48 lakhs was made as subsidy to be disbursed among these families by DRDA (@ Rs 6.00 lakhs per block) in addition to this Khadi & Village Industries Board and DIL sanctioned a subsidy of Rs 4.800 lakhs and Scheduled Castes development corporation gave a subsidy of Rs 9.721 lakhs. Besides this, a sum of Rs 69.746 lakhs was proposed as loan by the financial institutions for the benefit of the target groups.

(*b*) *Achievements*: Actual performance exceeded the targets fixed for this period This shows the enthusiasm and a sense at commitment to this programme of executing agency. Rs 49.64 lakhs were leased by DRDA Sikar as subsidy against the target of Rs 48.00 lakhs. Actual disbursement exceeded the released amount by Rs 1.64 lakhs. The actual disbursement during this period as subsidy amount by DRDA Sikar comes to Rs 51.28 lakhs. In addition to this Rs 13.73 lakhs were spent on disbursement in the form of enhanced subsidy out of the Scheduled Castes development corporation's fund. The credit of Rs 84.03 lakhs was mobilised through financing institutions (Rs 53.31 lakhs from commercial banks and Rs 30.72 lakhs from cooperative banks). The allocation which was shown as Khadi and Village Industries Board and DIL subsidy of Rs 4.800 lakhs (as shown in Action plan of 1983-84 of IRDP, Sikar district) could not be received and disbursed.

It seems that under the IRD programme spacial efforts to uplift the living conditions of Scheduled Castes persons[5] and to help them cross the poverty line are being made in Sikar district.

(*xii*) *Block-wise Progress of IRD Programme During 1978-79 to 1983-84*

On examining the block-wise progress of IRD programme during 1978-79 to 1983-84 we find that the highest number of families benefited belonged to Panchayat Samities, Dhod where 915 families were given IRD benefits of Rs 10. 50. lakhs were disbursed as subsidy and the credit of Rs 19. 03 lakhs was mobilised for this purpose. Table 6.5 indicates block-wise details of persons benefited, subsidy disbursed and credit mobilised.

Loan and Subsidy Distributed Among The Year 1983-84: 4.41 per cent beneficiaries belonged to Scheduled Tribes while 50.38 per cent were from Scheduled Castes and 45.21 per cent beneficiaries belonged to other communities. On an average,a scheduled Tribe beneficiary was given benefit (subsidy/

5. Working Group of Modalities of Implementation of the Priority Sector lending and the Twenty-Point economic programme role of banks, Krishanaswamy working group, March, 1980.

TABLE 6.5: **Block-wise Progress of I.R.D. Programme During 1978-79 To 1983-84**

(*Rs in lakhs*)

Name of Block	*1978-79*			*1979-80*			*1980-81*		
	Total expenditure incurred	*Total credit mobilized*	*Total No. of families benefited*	*Total expenditure incurred*	*Total credit mobilized*	*Total No. of families benefited*	*Tatal expenditure incurred*	*Total credit mobilized*	*Total No. of families benefited*
1. Fatehpur	1.76	5.80	211	2.53	7.00	304	4.80	14 91	467
2. Srimadhopur	0.58	1.80	78	2.38	7.14	307	2.94	8.42	364
3. Danta Ramgarh	1.28	4.11	203	3.04	9.00	457	7.75	20.84	836
4. Neem-ka-Thana	0.93	2.85	90	3.54	11.35	450	6.57	19.34	749
5. Lachhmangarh	—	—	—	2.75	8.25	304	2.97	9.68	296
6. Dhod	—	—	—	—	—	—	3.07	7.70	279
7. Khandela	—	—	—	—	—	—	2.37	6.93	248
8. Piprali	—	—	—	—	—	—	2.59	8.40	283
Total for the District	4.55	14.56	582	14.24	42.74	1822	33.06	96.22	3522

(*Contd.*)

	1981-82			1982-83			1983-84		
	Total expenditure incurred	*Total credit mobilized*	*Total No. of families benefited*	*Total expenditure incurred*	*Total credit mobilized*	*Total No. of families benefited*	*Total expenditure incurred*	*Total credit mobilized*	*Total No. of families benefited*
1. Fatehpur	7.20	12.58	632	10.03	18.42	888	8.24	16.04	682
2. Srimadhopur	6.21	11.00	553	5.99	10.05	646	7.36	11.73	654
3. Danta Ramgarh	7.17	12.34	620	8.39	14.08	701	9.06	15.30	698
4. Neem-ka-Thana	8.72	13.60	678	7.50	11.49	661	4.83	8.17	490
5. Lachhamangarh	6.27	10.36	521	11.25	18.69	898	9.10	13.34	754
6. Dhod	4.29	7.34	369	10.46	18.30	952	10.50	19.03	915
7. Khandela	5.48	9.59	482	7.41	13.11	581	7.74	11.93	636
8. Piprali	4.36	7.22	363	6.89	10.62	556	7.92	13.53	613
Total for the district	49.70	84.03	4218	67.92	114.76	5883	68.21	109.07	5442

Source : Annual Action Plan 1984-85 (DRDA) District Rural Development Agency, Sikar, (Rajasthan).

loan) of Rs 3398 and Scheduled Caste beneficiary was given a benefit of Rs 3400 and beneficiary belonging to other caste was given benefit of Rs 3411. Table 6.6 clarifies the position of IRD benefit in Sikar district.

Table 6.6 shows that the highest subsidy component under IRDP was extended to beneficiaries belonging to Scheduled Castes and loan component was the highest in general category.

TABLE 6.6: **Loan and Subsidy Distributed During 1983-84**

(*Rs. in lakhs*

Castes	*No.*	*Percent-age*	*Subsidy*	*Scheduled Caste Dev. Corpora-tion Fund*	*Loan*	*Total benefit*
S.T.	186	4.41	3.16	—	3.16	6.32
S.C.	2125	50.38	22.40	13.73	36.13	72.26
Others	1907	45.21	20.31	—	44.74	65.05
Total	4218	100.00	45.87	13.73	84.03	143.63

Source: Annul Action Plan, 1984-85, DRDA, Sikar.

(*xiii*) *Findings*

Forty-eight villages spread over all in the Panchayat Samities of the district were surveyed to assess the working of IRDP during the year 1978-79 to 1983-84. 281 beneficiaries were contacted under this study. The findings are given in brief here :

(*a*) *Loan and Subsidy*: 993 applications were prepared for Rs 32.89 lakhs, banks sanctioned 862 loan applications amounting to Rs 16.91 lakhs.In 67.63 per cent cases the banks took more than a month's time to sanction the loan applications. DRDA released a sum of Rs 10.60 lakhs as subsidy for various purposes. In 63.98 per cent cases the DRDA took more than a month's time in the release of subsidy.

(*b*) *Selection*: By and large the prescribed procedure for indentification of IRD beneficiaries was followed in some cases it has been observed that the names of beneficiaries other than those selected were entertained. It was observed that 30.60 per cent beneficiaries were above the poverty line as per the prescribed norms, who in fact were not eligible to be a beneficiary.

(*c*) *Awareness About Insurance*: It was observed that most of the beneficiaries were not aware of the insurance scheme and as such they did not submit their claims. And even those claims were not attended to which were submitted.

(*d*) *Recovery Position*: The recovery position as reported by financial institutions is alarmingly poor. As on 31st July, 1983 a sum of Rs 2.56 lakhs was recovered in 48 villages from IRD beneficiaries and an amount of Rs 9.77 lakhs was due towards beneficiaries. Under IRD programme, 10 per cent rate of interest is chargeable but in some cases it was reported that the banks were charging more than the prescribed interest rate.

(*e*) *Indentification of Benefit Units*: It was observed that the specific need and economic potential of the beneficiaries and the area to which a person belongs was not given due weightage in allotment of economic activities in benefit unit. Hence, such persons do not get the real benefit of this programme.

(*f*) *Impact*: Out of 281 persons selected for the study, 195 were actually below proverty line whereas 86 possessed more than the prescribed income limit. During the year 1983-84, out of 195 persons who were below the proverty line, 68 persons crossed the poverty line after being benefited by this programme and 127 persons remained below the proverty line even after IRD benefits were extended to them.

Fifty-five beneficiaries of these forty-eight villages were contacted and their benefit units were physically verified. Out of 55 IRDP beneficiaries, 30 beneficiaries were in possession of complete units which were provided to them under this programme, while 13 beneficiaries were in partial possession of units and only 12 beneficiaries had no unit available in their possession.

It was observed that 2 goat units, 3 she-buffaloes units, 2 sheep units, 2 camel cast units, 1 tea shop unit, 1 barbar shop unit and 1 kirana shop unit were not in possession of the beneficiaries at the time of sample checking.

Most of the beneficiaries indicated that it was not possible to get loan and subsidy without using unfair means. This indicates the amount of corruption prevalent among block officials/ veterinary officials, bank officials and Sarpanch.

Here it would not be out of context to quote a case of Ramgarh village where a poor IRD beneficiary was suffering from leprosy. He had no assets of any kind. Benefit unit also could not be retained by him and whatever money he got by selling out this unit, was consumed in his treatment. He was a conscious God fearing person and had the feeling of sin for not being able to repay the bank loan. The investigating team feels that in such cases DRDA (District Rural Development Agency) should be given powers to write off the bank loan.

In some villages it was observed that the banks were charging a higher rate of interest than what was permissible, when the bank officials were approached about this, they pointed out that it being an incidental charge was permissible under rules. The matter was brought to the notice of NABARD, which took corrective steps.

Beneficiaries of one village complaint that the officials of Shekhawati Gramin Bank, Dhod have taken Rs 50 per thousand as bribe at the time of advancement of loan. This was also conceded by the Block Development Officer and Sarpanch of the village who were present at the time of sample checking. However, this needs further investigation.

Yet in other village an identified beneficiary complained that neither he was advanced the sanctioned loan, nor was any unit provided to him but he served with a notice by CC bank, to repay the loan. In this case it seems that the Sarpanch of the village was involved in maladjustment of loan and subsidy. This case requires further investigation.

It was also brought to the notice that a lady teacher of

Jaipur was selected in yet another village under this programme.

(g) *Suggestions*: With a view to solving these problems a few suggestions are mentioned here:

1. Identification of beneficiaries should be done strictly as per government guidelines. It is suggested that instead of the yearly selection of beneficiaries by Gram Sabha, income census of villages may be conducted and all the potential beneficiaries may be indentified. Their priority on the basis of extent of poverty may be fixed in Gram Sabha.
2. A procedure may be evolved to ensure the availability of provided units with the beneficiaries. Beneficiaries should not be allowed to shift their residence from one village to another, unless the loan is repaid. The list of the beneficiaries and benefits extended to them may be given wider publicity in the surrounding areas.
3. Purchases outside the district should be encouraged to prevent the fake transactions.
4. Adequate veterinary facilities should be provided in every village. Here it is suggested that Village Level Workers may be given elementary training in veterinary science, to provide urgent on-the-spot relief to the beneficiaries in every village. Users clubs may be constituted and a young beneficiary may be entrusted with the responsibility of checking and reporting the veterinary requirements to the VLW immediately. He may be given some allowance for the duty.
5. Banks may be asked to revise their repayment schedules. Recovery instalments may be reduced and they should be spread over a longer period, so as to leave a part of increased income with the beneficiaries.
6. In some hard cases, DRDA and banks may be given powers to write off the loan.
7. Extension work regarding IRD programme should be carried out and IRD beneficiaries may be imparted education about this programme. In this connection, 2 to 3 days beneficiary training camps at block level may be organised.

8. Limit of poverty line may be raised from Rs 700 per person per year to at least Rs 1000 per person per year looking to the decreasing value of money.
9. It was observed that beneficiaries belonging to remote areas retain their benefit units where as beneficiaries in road side village misuse it, so it is suggested that more benefits be extended in remote areas.
10. Proper marketing arrangements for products of benefit units may be made. In this connection, it is suggested that small show-rooms may be opened in nearby towns. These show-rooms could be managed by the co-operative societies of beneficiaries.
11. IRD beneficiaries who have been provided with the beneficiaries who have been provided with the buffalo or cow units should be allowed to stay with the potential benefit unit for 7 days. Banks should make payment to the seller of such units after 7 days of purchases. Banks may also be asked to obtain OK report from beneficiary before making payment. This system will ensure the quality of animal and will avoid artficial increase in milk production and as such high cost paid for such animals.

2. National Rural Employment Programme (NREP)

In April 1977, Food for Work Programme was launched with a view to generating additional employment apportunities especially in the rural areas.[6] Despite all sorts of financial and political support the programme could not reach the desired heights. It was in this context that a need to revamp and restructure the programme was felt and the concept of National Rural Employment Programme is the outcome of this thinking. The food for work programme was restructed and renamed as the National Rural Employment Programme from October, 1980.

(*i*) *Objectives*

The National Rural Employment Programme is a regular part of the Sixth and Fifth Five Year Plans with effect from 1st

6. National Rural Employment Programme.

April, 1981, the programme is being implemented as a centrally sponsored scheme on 50:50 share basis between the Centre and the States. Wages are depending upon possibilities, paid partly in cash and partly as gain. Mobile fair price shops are organised at the centres where rural works are in progress so that cloth, vegetable oil, salt and other basic requirements can be made available. The programme has three basic objectives:

1. Generation of additional gainful employment for the employed and underemployed persons both men and women in rural areas;
2. Creation of durable community assets for strengthening rural infrastructure which will lead to the rapid growth of rural economy.
3. Improvement of the nutritional status and the living standard of the rural poor.

Works to be Undertaken Under the Programme

The works which directly help in strengthening the rural iufrastructure and result in creation of durable community assets in the rural areas and also those works which improve the rural economy and the standard of life in villages can be taken up under the programme. The types of works that can be taken up under the programme are as under:

1. Aforestation and social forestry on government and community lands including lands, belonging to local bodies like Panchayat, etc. road-side plantation, plantation along canal banks, on wastelands, and on the sides of railway lines, other land unfit for cultivation, plantation of fuel, fodder and fruit.
2. Construction of drinking water wells, community irrigation wells, group housing and land development projects for Scheduled Castes and tribes.
3. Construction of water tanks and repairing deepening and rejuvenation of existing tanks to provide water for human use and cattle.
4. Minor irrigation works including those relating to flood protection, drainage and anti-waterlogging works, construction of intermediate and main drain field

channels and land levelling, etc. in the command areas of irrigation projects, cleaning of water courses, etc.

5. Soil and water consevation and land reclamation.
6. Rural roads subject to standard specification, where specific financial provision exist, for their hard surfacing cross drainage, maintenance, etc., and
7. Construction of school and balwadi buildings, panchayat ghars, communi y centres, drinking water wells, drinking water sources for the wild animals in forest areas, cattle ponds, pinjrapoles, gaushalas, bathing and washing platforms, community toilets, community garbage pits, community bio-gas plants.

(*ii*) *Progress and Assessment*

The wage under this programme will be paid partly in food grains and partly in cash. 1 kg. of foodgrain per head per day may be given as part of the wages in foodgrains and the balance amount may be paid in cash. The foodgrains will be supplied to workers at subsidised rates. The rates per kg. will be Rs. 1.50 for wheat, Rs 1.85 for common rice and Rs 2.10 for superfine rice. Actual performance exceeded the targets fixed. This shows the enthusiasm and a sense of commitment to this programme of executing agency. Rs 21.00 lakhs were released by DRDA, Sikar against the target of Rs 20 lakhs in the year 1983-84. Actual disbursement exceeded the released amount by 1.00 lakh. 2.35 lakhs labour days were targetted by DRDA, Sikar against this programme in the year 1984-85. Actual achievement exceeded the targetted labour days in the ame year by 2.45 lakhs labour days. In terms of percentage this achievement is related to 104 per cent. Contribution of this programme to Rajasthan's rural employment programme is considerable. Sikar district's actual performance exceeded rather than other backward districts. Hence, this programme is still good rather better in its over all assessment.

(*iii*) *Swaminathan Report*

Working group was constituted under the Chairmanship of Mr M.S. Swaminathan to review the performance of the NREP. The group in its report submitted in April 1982 recommended that NREP should be given a very high priority in the allocation of resources and in the attention given by the State Governments for allevation of poverty in the country.

3. Desert Development Programme (DDP)

The district is situated in the north-eastern desert zone of the State and is characterised by frequent drought and famine conditions. Main occupation of the population is agriculture. The desert development programme was started in the district from 1977-78 as a sequal to the recommendation of the National Commission on Agriculture to check desertification. Efforts have been made to tackle the problems of the desert on the fronts of soil and water conservation[7]. The programme has made a distinct impact on the developmental process of the economy of the district. Expenditure of Rs 1061.76 lakhs has been incurred under the programme since its inception up to 1983-84. The desert development programme was started as 100 per cent centrally sponsored scheme but from 1979-80, the funding pattern was changed to 50:50 basis amongst states and Centre. The programme is administered through DPAP/ IRDP.

(i) Progress and Assessment

Sector wise financial and physical achievements and impact of the programme during the years 1980-81 to 1983-84.

Expenditure of Rs 349.12 lakhs and Rs 157.61 lakhs was incurred under the programme during the period 1980-81 to 1983-84 as per details given in Table 6.7.

Sectorwise financial and physical progress has been narrated as so on.

1. *Agriculture*

(*a*) *Soil Survey*: Unless this scheme expenditure of Rs 14.63 lakhs was incurred during the period of 1980 to 1983. Reconnaissance survey in 408 thousand hectares was conducted. In addition 6700 soil samples were analysed by the Mobile Soil Survey Unit. 25 spriknler irrigation sets were distributed for

7. K.V. Patel, *Structure of Farm and Resource Use in Drought Prone Areas*, National Institute of Bank Management, Bombay, 1978, Vol. II.

demonstration topographical survey was also made for 5000 hectares.

TABLE 6.7 : **Sector-wise Financial and Physical Achievements During 1980-81 to 1983-84**

(Rs in Lakhs)

S.No.	*Sector*	*Expenditure incurred during 1980 to 1983*	*Actual Expenditure 1983*	*Total*
1.	Agriculture	39.2	21.0	60.2
2.	Ground water	50.7	64.3	115.0
3.	Irrigation	60.9	8.7	69.6
4.	Forestry	78.5	35.8	114.3
5.	Sheep Development	6.8	4.1	10.9
6.	Cattle and dairy	22.0	—	22.0
7.	Power	51.9	—	51.9
8.	Animal husbandry	20.4	15.1	35.5
9.	Cattle drinking water	1.0	3.9	4.9
10.	Agency and execution	11.1	4.7	15.8
11.	Small farmer development agency	2.2	—	2.2
12.	Co-operative	1.3	—	1.3

Source: Office of the District Rural Developmeut Agency, Sikar.

(*b*) *Soil Conservation*: Expenditure of Rs 24.53 lakhs was incurred for the period of 1980 to 1983 under this sector. Work was under progress in 5 water sheds which were sanctioned during the period out of 3 units, 2 units of soil conservation department were abolished since September 1982. At present, one office of Deputy Director and one unit of soil conservation are functioning in the district.

2. *Ground Water*

Under this scheme, Rs 50.7 lakhs were spent during 1980 to

1983. 930 well inventories, 991 chemical analysis of water sample were done and 202 geographical sounding tests, 7 exploratory bore holes, 3 obarrations wells and 1 pump set were done together with the collection of 919 water samples.

3. *Irrigation*

Under the irrigation sector, Rs 609 lakhs were incurred during 1980-1983. In addition, 11 schemes were also sanctioned. Two more schemes namely Chhanjana and Mimki were sanctioned. Thus out of the remaining 15 schemes, 7 schemes namely, Surana, Sagar ki Mari, Baran, Hironwari, Dhani, Paran, Kotaki Nagal, Hardas ka Bas, were completed during this period. The remaining 4 schemes namely Ranasar Jeelo, Dokan, and Nimki were under progress.

4. *Forestry*

Under this sector, Rs 78.5 lakhs were incurred during 1980-1983. The maintenance work of 4 nurseries was continued under the village fuel wood and fodder plantation follow up, plantation and advance action was done in 450 hectares. 130 thousand plants were distributed and advance action was taken for raising 100 thousand plants. Follow up action under mixed plantation was done in 400 hectares. Maintenance work of plants in 400 hectares under mixed plantation was done.

5. *Sheep Development*

Sheep breeding is one of the important occupations of the rural people. Under this sector total expenditure incurred was lakhs during 1980-1983. As regard performance, 280 sheep breeders were trained in 8 camps. Funds were also sanctioned to the Ram Distribution Farm, Fatehpur for the purchase of deshi sheep of Nali and Chokla breed. A cross-breeding programme with the Russian Marino ramsw as envisaged to have more cross-breed rams/lambs. At present, farm at Fatehpur, 845 crossbreed rams distributed. Pasture development was undertaken in 500 hectares and lambing was 1270.

6. *Dairy*

The expenditure incurred under this sector was Rs 22.0 lakhs, during the period from 1980 to 1983. The average collection of milk per day was 1.93 thousand litres, 18 dairy cooperative societies were established during this period. No provision for dairy sector was kept in the year 1982-83.

7. *Power*

Power is one of the basic requirements for various developmental programmes. The total funds transferred to RSES for the period 1980 to 1983 amounted to Rs 51.9 lakhs. During this period, 130 villages were electrified and 1023 wells were energised. The Kotputli-Neem-ka-Thana 132 KV line was under progress.

8. *Animal Husbandry*

Under this sector the total expenditure incurred was Rs 20.4 lakhs during 1980-1983. Eight more animal health centres, namely Kirdoli, Chiplota, Kasikabus, Shishu, Dirvala, Kudan, Balahan, and Kanwat were established. During this period two Gaushalas were sanctioned grants for cattle development. One mobile animal health centre was also established in the district. Besides this 4 existing centres and one surra control unit was also maintained.

9. *Drinking Water for Cattle*

In the desert area, scarcity of drinking water is not a problem only for human beings but also for cattles. Looking to the need of the area it was decided during 1981-82 to take up schemes for this purpose through PHED to solve this problem. During the year 1983-84 Rs 3.9 lakhs were actually spent while during the period from 1980 to 1983 Rs 1.0 lakhs were incurred. There is ample scope for such schemes in the interior areas of the district.

10. *Agency and Execution*

District Rural Development Agency is wholly responsible for the execution and progress of desert development programmes. During the period of 1980-81 to 1983-84, Rs 11.4 lakhs were incurred while the actual expenditure was only Rs 4.7 lakhs.

Under this programme 26 sheep units, 35 goat units, 87 milch cattles, 83 bullock camel carts and 25 bullocks/camels were distributed during 1980-1983. 158 dry furming demonstrations were organised. Subsidy was also provided for a pump set and 14 wells/tube wells. During this period Rs 2.2 lakhs were spent for providing subsidy with the advent of IRDP, these facilities have now been merged with that programme since 1981. Now no funds are being provided for this purpose.

11. *Co-Operative*

To meet the credit requirements of the people and strengthen the co-operative institutions, expenditure of Rs 1.3 lakhs was incurred during the period 1980-81 to 1983-84.

4. Special Livestock Production Programme (SLPP)

Under the new IRDP this programme has been merged. Outlay required for this programme will be met out of the overall provisions made for Integrated Rural Development Programme.

5. Training of Rural Youth for Self-Employment (TRYSEM)

The seeds of the national scheme of training of rural youth for self-employment (TRYSEM) were sown in August 1979. The principal objective was the removal of unemployment among youth. The scheme aims at providing necessary skills and technology to the rural youth to enable them to take up self-employment. Initially, it was proposed to train rural youth every year, both in IRD and non-IRD areas. Even after the extension of IRDP to all the blocks, TRYSEM is to continue as a separate scheme with separate financial allocations so as to strengthen the training infrastructure.

The strategy for training includes, apart from institutional training, training through local seericing and industrial units, master-craftsman, artisans and skilled workers. During the period of training, the trainees are also given financial assistance. The trainees are also entitled, in suitable cases, to a free tool kit, costing Rs 250.

Under TRYSEM programme 154 youths were imparted training in various trades in Sikar district. Out of 154 youths, who were trained under TRYSEM, 47 belonged to Scheduled Castes, 4 to Scheduled Tribes and 103 to other communities. Under this scheme, 97 youths were provided wage/se.

TABLE 6.8: **Trade-wise Break-up of TRYSEM Trainees During the Year 1983-84**

S, No.	*Trade*	*No. of youths trained*	*No. of trained youths provided wage/self-employ ment*	*Youth under training*
1.	Motor binding	13	5	52
2.	House wiring	5	3	5
3.	General mechanic	—	1	1
4.	Pebe fitting	—	—	—
5.	Cycle repairing	1	3	4
6.	Tailoring	78	55	208
7.	Kashida	26	4	34
8.	Auto engineers	—	1	1
9.	Press compositors	6	4	3
10.	Knitting	2	2	12
11.	Galicha	7	6	4
12.	Bundi Bandhana	1	2	1
13.	Radio mechanic	—	—	1
14.	Turner welding	5	3	3
15.	Dari marking	—	—	—
16.	Zildsaj	—	—	—
17.	Soap making	2	2	2
18.	Gota industries	2	2	2
19.	Watch repair	2	1	2
20.	Shoe making	4	3	4
21.	Reja weaving	—	—	3
22.	Motor driving	—	—	10
23.	Blanket making	—	—	—
	Total	154	57	349

Source: Office of the District Rural Development, Sikar, Rajasthan.

employment during the year 1983-84. There were 340 youths who were received training in various trades by the end of 31st March, 1983 in the district. Table 6.8 shows trade-wise break-up of TRYSEM trainees during the year 1983-84.

Table 6.8 indicates that the majority of youths have been given training in tailoring and got wage/self-employment. It seems that the marketing potential of this trade is higher in comparison to other trade because it is attracting increasing number of youths.

(*i*) *Progress and Assessment*

Actual performance exceeded the targets fixed for this programme. This shows the enthusiasm and a sense of commitment for this programme of executing agency. About 200 families in each block under rural artisans and TRYSEM sector will be benefited. Thus about 1675 families are likely to be benefited under this programme. The total financial advancement of Rs 38.62 lakhs has been worked out along with the IRD subsidy of Rs 14.85 lakhs.

7

Suggestions and Conclusions

After having surveyed the various aspects of the socio-economic rural life of the Sikar district, now it is for us to submit a resume of the whole of it in order to draw some useful suggestions and come to concrete and constructive conclusions.

1. Physical Features

Sikar district with a vast area of 7732 square kilometres covers 2.02 per cent of the total area of Rajasthan. The district is for the most part, levelled and fertile, though sandy to a large extent. The soil ranges rocky in the south-west and black in the eastern and southern parts, but the sandy soil is most abundent. The streams flowing in this district are of non-perennial nature. The climate of the region is dry and healthy but is marked by extreme variations of temperature during the summer and the winter. The average rainfall of the district is 460.9MM, but widely divergent precipitation has been recorded in different tehsils. The problem of soil erosion has assumed serious proportions at certain places and the vast areas have been rendered useless by it. The important minerals of the district are mica, scapstone, glass sand, iron ore, felsper and building stones. As the industries consuming these minerals have not developed in Sikar district, a large part of the mineral production has to be sent to other parts of the State and the country. However, there is great scope for developing cement, glass, ceramic, tiles, electrical goods and line manufacturing industries in this district. A detailed survey should be carried out by the mining department regarding the mineral wealth of this district.

The district occupies a prominent place in the production of the minerals especially the non-metallic minerals. Among the matallic minerals, copper is the most important mineral which has been found out at Parida, Neema-ka-Thana. In addition to this stones used for building purposes are found all over the district.

The soil survey works were started in Sikar district during the year 1977-78. The detailed soil survey is normally carried out in the areas affected by soil erosion and having good agricultural potential. It recommends about better soil and water management.

The forest area in Sikar district is not much significant from the point of view of forest production. Thorny and spiky bushes are found in the marginal lands. The savannah type of vegetation is found in plains which are sandy. This species is especially useful for grass production.

The district is what may be regarded as a broder-line case with regard to the satisfactory agricultural conditions. In the absence of wide spread irrigation facilities, the suitability of the district with regard to normal agriculture has to be judged. The irrigated area constituted 19.80 per cent of the total net area sown during the year 1983-84.

The outstanding feature of the crop pattern in Sikar district is its wide variety of crops, abundance of food crops over non-food crops. Kharif is the main crop of the district. 85.66 per cent area was utilised for cereals.

Tenancy in the state is governed by Rajasthan Tenancy Act 1955. It is one of the most important and progressive laws relating to the agrarian reforms. There are various classes of tenants as, (a) Khatedar, (b) Malik, (c) Tenant of Khudkast, and (d) Gair khatedar tenant. Every cultivator is either a tenant or a subtenant or an allottee or a trespasser.

According to the livestock census 1977, the total livestock population of the district was 1361092 lakhs. There were 12 veterinary hospitals, 4 veterinary health contres, 3 veterinary dispensaries, and 2 mobile veterinary units in the district. In 1957 the forest rules were enforced in the district in order to protect the wild life in the forest areas.

The consumption pattern of electricity shows a fairly good use of power for agriculture purposes. The domestic consumption of power in Sikar district was 7.666 million KWH in 1983-84. Among all a very significant rise has been marked in irrigation from 39.111 million KWH in 1980-81 to 134.480 milion KWH in 1983-84.

Although there are no large scale industries in the district, yet due to favourable geographical situation regarding availability of raw material in huge quantity, there were 148 registered factories in the district during the year 1983-84. The district appears to have a bright future of industrial development.

The district is an exporter of industrial raw material besides foodgrains mainly bajara, moth, moong, gawar, powder, limestone, dolomite, and quartz are exported from this district. All the tahsils and block headquarters are getting the advantage of banking facilities.

As far as the transport is concerned, the district has a satisfactory net work of all weather roads. All the block headquarters are linked with the district headquarter with pacca roads. One national highway and three State highways pass through the district. The plans are under preparation of connecting villages with the population of 3000 to 4000 by roads. With regard to the telegraph facilities the district had 451 post offices, 18 telegraph offices and 13 telephone exchanges in the year 1983-84.

The district had 531 co-operative societies of various types in 1983-84. There was a central co-operative bank, total membership of the co-operative societies stood to 178780, share capital to Rs 128 lakhs and working capital to Rs 1042 lakhs during 1983-84. Loans worth Rs 463.95 lakhs were advanced during this period.

2. Physical Features and Population Pattern

The population of Sikar district was 1377245 in 1981. It has a density of 178 persons per square kilometre. As only 49.04 per cent of the total population is females, there is a majority of males in sex distribution. However, this characteristic is found in other neighbouring districts as well as in Rajasthan. A study of civil condition shows that the percentage of unmarried females in the rural sector was much lower than the percentage of unmarried males. The position is just the reverse in case of married females. Child marriage is still prevalent in the district. The rate of growth of population is expected to be higher in the next five years. The pressure on land is quite heavy in this district as comparedto other districts of Rajasthan. Out of the total population, 278936 persoas constituting 20.25 per cent of the total population lived in the urban areas of tbe district. Since 1901 the sex ratio has remained almost steady. In the rural areas the ratio has shown a steady rise since 1901. As in the rest of the country agriculture is the main occupation of the rural majority of the people in this region. At the district level, 69.16 per cent of the population comprises non-workers, 24.67 per cent workers and the remaining 6.22 per cent marginal workers. There is a lesser number of workers as well the marginal workers in the urban areas as compared to the rural areas both among males as compared to females.

Education

Of the total population, 25.43 per cent of people were literate in Sikar district in 1981. The percentage of literates in the rural sector of this district was only 22.43 in 1981. The proportion of literate males and literate females in the rural sector was 38.28 per cent and 6.01 per cent respectively. The present facilities for education in the rural areas of the district are inadequate, there being only one primary school for an average population of about 2000 persons. It is in the light of the meagre number of schools that more schools should be opened so as to reach the general target of one primary school for an average population of 1000 persons.

The type of education imparted in primary schools is not of much use to the children of the rural folk as it does not help them pursue agriculture more efficiently and fruitfully. The important features of basic schools should be introduced in primary schools which should develop the spirit of self-help in them. The courses should be so remodelled as may make the rural children better farmers or better craftsmen. Schools should be closed for at least a fortnight during the sowing and harvesting seasons so that the children may share the workload of their parents in the fields. The shortage of equipments, books and stationery, etc. should also be made up.

Medical Facilities

The hospitals and allopathic dispensaries are mostly located in towns and serve the urban dwellers. For rural population, ayurvedic dispensaries have proved to be more serviceable. They have a cheaper system of treatment and the medicines can easily be prepared at home. At present, there is one such dispensary for 10,000 persons. The Government should increase the number of Ayurvedic dispensaries and should give more grants for medicines. It can now be safely said that the government should increase the number of Ayurvedic institutions in the rural areas and should provide more grants for medicines.

3. Land Utilisation and Crop Pattern

The well-being of agricultural population depends upon land and its proper use. The land use pattern has been presented under the five headings—forest, land put to non-agricultural uses, barren and uncultivable land, other uncultivated land excluding fallow land, fallow lands and the net area sown. A general conclusion can well be drawn that the area under forest figures during the planning perio d is the unexpected change in it from year to year.

This is due to the changing defi nition of forest adopted by the office of the Director of Land Records from time to time.

The forest policy resolution suggests a forest cover of 60 per cent of the area in hilly regions and 20 per cent in plains. The forest should be expanded and the best way in our opinion is the creation of farm forest. At present, large blocks of land are lying as waste in rural areas in the name of pasture land but virtually these grow nothing.

The area under permanent pasture and other grazing lands increased steadily from year to year. The average land under tree crops and groves also showed a growing tendency during the planning period. Land under tree crops and groves is certainly a very welcome and encouraging trend.

The fall in the area of cultivable waste show that more land has been brought under cultivation or has been utilised for pasture or other groves.

The main purpose of keeping land as fallow is to enable it to recoup its fertility of which is lost by repeated raising of crops. Other fallow lands are those lands which are left uncultivated for a period exceeding one year but less than five years. The reason for keeping those lands fallow for such a long period are many and varied. Some of the important causes are poverty of cultivators, inadequate supply of water, silting up of canals and rivers, etc. Most of the causes have either been removed with the advancement in the science of agricultural chemistry and soil technology. It can, therefore, be safely expected that a major portion of fallow land can be brought under cultivation with the help of modern scientific methods of agriculture and increase in irrigation facilities.

In 1980-81, the area under this head was 493878 hectares which showed an upward trend. There was sharp increase in it during 1983-84 and it increased to 523270 hectares. The increase in the net area sown represents a growth of 82.15 per cent.

The outstanding features of the crop pattern in Sikar district is its wide variety of crops. The crops have been broadly classified under five heads. Cereals, pulses, sugarcane, cotton and oilseeds. Among cereals, the only other important crop is wheat. In 1980-81, the area under pulses was 5909 hectares. It increased to 12843 in 1983-84 over those years of time. The only important commercial crop of the district is groundnut which is sown on 2974 hectares in 1983-84. The production of crop was 2662 tonnes in 1983-84.

One of the important functions of the agriculture department is to motivate the farmers for adoption of better farming techniques and educate them in the use of scientific means of agriculture.

The district is largely a single crop area, but on lands which are irrigated by wells, the high yielding varieties are also used. In such cases one year rotation is followed which is like this: hybrid bajra plus moong mauth followed by wheat

Sikar district has an average rainfall of 460.9 mm. Areas getting an annual rainfall of less than 50 cms are generally not regarded as 'suitable for normal agriculture. There is no large scale facility in Sikar district and agriculture depends mainly on wells, tanks and such other sources. As wells are the most important source of irrigation in this district, it is very necessary that new wells should be dug and old wells be kept in proper state after repairs. There are no perennial rivers in the district.

This is a happy sign in the context of the food problem of

the country. However, it is well known that the cultivation of non-food crops brings better returns to the farmers. What is needed is a balanced agricultural policy in which food crops and non-food crops, both may occupy their proper place to provide a scientific rotation of crops. Enquiries and group discussions with the rural folk and with the experts in the field of agricultural technology brought us to the conclusion that no large scale readjustment in the present cropping pattern was possible without a simultaneous expansion in the irrigation facilities. The state Government should launch an extensive programme for the production of major crops, consumption of more fruits, vegetables, and provide the necessary facilities. There has not been any significant shift from one crop to another. However, there has been a definite shift in preference for hybrid seeds from the conventional seeds.

There is no doubt that the yield of crops can increase considerably if proper irrigation facilities can be made available. Efforts should be made to construct new wells in large numbers and deepen the existing wells.

The use of pumping sets could be popularised by block development authorities or Panchayats.

In order to have properly irrigated crops, the optimum quantity of water should be applied to the crops. For this, it is necessary to know the water requirements of each crop. There is a mistaken belief among cultivators that the larger is the quantity of water applied to the crops, the better is the yield. But too much watering harms the plants.

Efforts should also be made to conserve rain water by construction of small tanks in areas wherever possible. The beds of these tanks can be utilised for growing crops after they get dry.

4. Rural Indebtedness and Rural Finance

Rural indebtedness and rural finance are the co-related financing problems. While the former tells the story relating to the problems of loans that have already been entrusted to the rural people, the latter makes one aware of the problems connected with financing of the rural people.

The rural indebtedness has been presented under two heads: The agriculture sector and the non-agriculture sector. The percentage of the agriculture sector's indebtedness is higher than that of the non-agriculture sector, i.e. 57.25 per cent in the agriculture sector.

The main source of loans is the moneylender in rural areas. The cooperative societies or other government agencies have not made much advances in this sector.

Because of heavy pressure on land the per capita income of major portion of population is low. People are not able to earn enough to meet the expenditure. Thus, pressure on land is the main cause of rural indebtedness. In addition to the main cause of indebtedness, the debt of today is the debt of yesterday and the chief obstacle in the way of relief is the attitude of the poorer classes towards this customary feature of their life. Some of the main causes responsible for rural indebtedness are ; the ancestral debt, illiteracy of farmers, traditional link, vagaries of the climatic condition and such other calamities, liberal financing, a high rate of interest, and lack of adequate marketing facilities, lack of funds and depressed mentality of the farmer lead to lesser productivity of his load.

At times, various corrective measures have been suggested to overcome these problems. Some of them are to remove the need for borrowing, protecting the assets of agriculture from passing into the hands of moneylenders, and it is essential to assess the quantum of resources likely to be available in the district for successful implementation of the district credit plan.

One of the most important sources of resource is availability by the accreation of deposits. Other important source of resource availabity is recycling of funds.

In this district, over all, recovery position of commercial banks including RRB is rather poor. One of the main reasons for poor performance on the recovery front is the top-sided development of the agricultural loan portfolio, with predominance of either short-term loans or medium-term loans. In certain areas branches have not provided short-term crop loans to those who have availed themselves of the medium-term facility. Either situation is harmful in a way. When crop loans are not given to borrowers, enjoying term loan facility, for containing funds for crop cultivation, which is recurring annual need, they approach other sources. Since the annual repayment of short term loans is a must for getting the facility renewed every year, the borrower owes allegiance primarily to the purveyor of short-term credit. If elements go against expectations and unfavourable to the borrower, he does not have immediately to face the repercussions of such a default. On the other hand, when investment loans are not extended adequately in an area, the farm development suffers. In such a situation, if the crop fails due to natural factors, the borrower who has been availing himself of only short-term credit, finds it difficult to stage a come back in subsequent years, by farming on his land which has no development-oriented investment done on it. One simple way to rectify this situation is that lending banks should take care of both the short-term and medium credit needs of borrowers.

It is needless to say that appropriate measures need to be taken soon by the banks and the State Government for bringing to heed the mounting overdues and improving the recovery rate.

Causes of Rural Indebtedness

Some of the main causes for rural indebtedness can be categorised as under:

1. The ancestral debt
2. Private moneylenders live in the locality of borrowers
3. Vagaries of the climatic condition and other calamities
4. Litigation
5. Liberal financing
6. A high rate of interest, and
7. Lack of adequate marketing facilities is another factor.

To overcome these problems, the following steps may be taken to provide debt relief to the rural poor :

1. To remove the need for borrowing
2. Protecting the assets of agriculturist from passing into the hands of moneylenders
3. To implement the Rural Credit Survey Committee's recomendations
4. To provide rural finance facilities, and
5. Proper marketing facilities,

5. Rural Industrialisation

Cottage and village industries provide the subsidiary source of income to the rural population. Such industries also keep the people employed during the period they are not engaged in agriculture. It has been estimated on the basis of the sample study that there is under-employment and disguised unemployment in the agricultural sector.

Some of the weavers engaged in handloom industry have formed cooperative societies. In order to promote production, Government should make the raw material and finance available to co-operative societies.

Leather industry engages backward and low-caste people. This industry has three branches: Tanning, charas-making and shoe-making. The quality of tanned hides is poor because scientific methods are not adopted. Charas-making requires higher investment than the shoe-making. Consequently, the choice of specialising in chars or shoe-making depends on the money a person has in his pocket. Charas-making secures a larger profit to the workers. The shoe-makers work with obsolete tools and techniques, and therefore, there is urgent need for starting training-cum-production centres to improve their lot.

Bullocks provide the draught power in a village 'ghani'. The village 'ghanies' can function well only when there is a steady supply of oilseeds. Steps need be taken to help ghani- to procure the seeds for normal work. The problem of storage of oilseeds and sheds over 'ghanis' also need attention.

Carpenters and blacksmiths mostly do the repair work. There is considerable scope for manufacture of good quality agricultural implements but that will be possible only if adequate arrangements are made for training and supply of better type of tools.

Those industries which can be taken up by all without much training, such as hand-spinning, basket-making, rope and niwar making, bee-keeping and poultry farming, etc. should be encouraged by organising cooperative societies. For the industries which need properly trained workers, such as blacksmithy and carpentry the Government should open more training-cum-production centres. Model colonies with adequate facilities should be built up for such industries like flaying, tanning, charas-making and glue-making. Such colonies will provide healthy surroundings and contribute to increase the efficiency of workers.

Rural industrialisation provides clinical remedies to many socio-economic ills prevalent in the district. Village industries have a capacity to create more employment opportunities, balanced regional development, low cost of employment, full utilisation of local resources, amelioration of the agricultural labourers and mobilisation of savings.

Some important problems are being faced by these industries. Such as, non-availability of raw material, inadequate and exploitative market, shortage of finance, outmoded and traditional trchnology, competition with large scale industriesl and acute shortage of power. Beside these problems, the rura industries also face the problem of under-utilisation of their capacity.

With a wiew to solving these problems some suitable suggestions are made here. The Government should open more taining-cum-production centres. The industries department of the State Government should provide the technical know-how and the necessary equipments. Cooperative societies may be formed to look after the supply of raw material and the sale of the goods produced. Effective steps should be taken to check adulteration of oil by Ghanimen. The Panchayat/societies should be encouraged to penalies the defaulters. Supply of power should be regular. Loans should be made available to independent units by bringing them under cooperative fold. Competition with large-scale industries should be avoided as these small indutries are not capable of doing this.

Rural industrialisation is the only answer to remove rural poverty. It is not desirable to establish centralised industries which require large capital resources which are beyond the capacity of people living in villages. The problem of unemployment and under-employment will not be solved unless the cottage and village industries plan their effective role in the rural economy of the district.

It is, therefore, necessary to indentify various problems being faced by these industries :

1. Non-availability of raw material.
2. Inadequate and exploitative market.

3. Shortage of finance.
4. Outmoded and traditional technology.
5. Competition with large scale industries.
6. Problem of power.

With a view to solving these problems, a few suggestions are mentioned here :

1. The Government should open more training-cum-production centres.
2. Cooperative societies may be formed to look after the supply of raw material.
3. Supply of power should be regular.
4. Loans should be made available.
5. Competion with large scale industries should be avoided.

6. Rural Development Programmes

The India mostly lives in villages, is a cliche but it is as much true today as it was many centuries ago. Nearly 80 per cent of the rural population in the country depends on agriculture and allied activities for its livelihood.

The integrated rural development programme, in its present form, was launched in 1975 in 2300 selacted blocks all over the country and adding 300 blocks every year. The main objectives of the integrated rural development programmes are to raise families in the indentified target groups above the poverty line and create substantial additional opportunities of employment in the rural areas.

The primary purpose of this study has been to assess critically and evaluate the impact of this programme on economic conditions of persons below the poverty line and evaluate the extent to which they have fruitfully benefited.

Actual performance has exceeded the targets fixed for this period. This shows the enthusiasm and a sense of commitment to this programme of the existing agency. It seems that under this programme special efforts to uplift the living conditions of Scheduled Castes persons and to help them cross the poverty line are being made in the district.

Brief findings of the study, concerning the working of this programme are : 993 applications were prepared for Rs 32.89

lakhs. Bank sanctioned 862 loan applications for Rs 16.91 lakhs. 67.63 per cent cases the bank took more than a month's time to sanction the loan applications. By and large, the prescribed procedure for identification of IRD beneficiaries was followed but in some cases it has been seen that the names of beneficiaries other than the select list were excluded. It was observed that most of the beneficiaries were not aware of the insurance scheme. The recovery position as reported by financing institutions is alarmingly poor. Some persons crossed the poverty line after being beneficiaries that it was not possible to get loan and subsidy without using unfair means. In some villages it was observed that the banks were charging a higher rate of interest than what was permissible from IRD beneficiaries.

The integrated rural development programme is an enthusiastic centrally sponsored programme for accelerating the speed of rural recovery and ameliorating the lot of the rural poor. The success of the programme largely depends on the co-ordinated and active involvement of all the people. The success of programme should not be evaluated on the basis of the number of families to whom loan facilities have been extended but by the number of families whose income has increased to such an extent as to enable them to cross the poverty line.

In April 1977 the 'Food Programme' was launched with a view to generating additional employment opportunities especially in the rural areas.

Rs 21.00 lakhs were released by DRDA Sikar against the target of Rs 20.00 lakhs in the year 1983-84. Actual performance exceeded the targets fixed for this programme.

The NREP should receive a very high priority in the allocation of resources and in the attention given by the State governments for removing poverty in the country.

The district is situated in the north-eastern desert zone of the State and is characterised for frequent drought and famine conditions. The mainstay of the population is agriculture. The Desert Development Programme was started in the district from 1977-78 as as equal to the recommendation of the National Commission on Agriculture for checking the process of desertification.

The programme has made a distinct impact on the development process of the economy of the district. Expenditure of Rs 1061.76 lakhs has been incurred under the programme since the inception up to 1983-84. This programme was started as a 100 per cent centrally sponsored scheme but from 1976-80, the funding pattern was changed to 50:50 basis.

The seeds of the national scheme of training of rural youth for self-employment (TRYSEM) were sown in August 1979. The principal objective of the training was the removal of unemployment among youth.

Actual performance exceeded the targets fixed for this programme. About 200 families in each block under rural artisans and TRYSEM sector will be benefited. The total financial advancement of Rs 38.62 lakhs has been worked out involving the IRD subsidy of Rs 14.85 lakhs.

7. Suggestions and Conclusions

The rural sector is the most pre-dominant feature in the economic structure of India and the Economics of rural India has therefore to be understood in terms of real situation prevalent in the countryside. According to the latest census of 1981, more than 80 per cent of people live in villages. Agriculture continues to be an important occupation in rural India. The reasons for this belated realisation are very clear. Agriculture alone contributes to 40 per cent of the national income. It has rightly been said that in Sikar (Rajasthan) nothing moves unless agriculture moves. A slight neglect of agricultural sector spells doom. Sikar's economy (Rajasthan' economy also) is so much dependent on agriculture that it cannot face the impact of even one crop failure. During the year of crop failure which may be due to flood, drought or any other natural calamity the rural population has no marketable surplus which has the chain effect on all sectors of economy dependent on agriculture for raw material or for sale of consumer products to rural India.

The following measures should be taken to promote development of agriculture :

(a) Spread of literacy
(b) Spread of irrigation facilities
(c) Speedy implementation of land reforms
(d) Providing credit facilities, and
(e) Spread of cooperative movement.

These are the major requirements to raise production and productivity.

One of the basic objectives of economics as a social science is to help in the decision-making process. By the same token, a study of rural economics aims at improving the decision-making process of all concerned with the material welfare of the rural society. Besides, the realisation about political relevance and social implications of neglecting or otherwise of the rural areas, the rural sector is recognised for its economic potential. Rural development, therefore, has become an integral part of public policy. A stream of development programmes is devised by the governments for the purpose. The actual outcome of the programmes is appreciated and assimilated by the millions of rural people spread over the width and breadth of rural Sikar (Rajasthan). The analysis of decision-making proccess of the rural people would help the policy-makers in devising and revising the programmes to achieve rural development.

All these programmes will have to be continued in the Seventh Five Year Plan in view of their importance. However, some problems in implementation of these programmes will have to be tackled if full benefits are to be derived from the high investment which would be made under these programmes in the period 1985-90 :

1. *Lack of People's Involvement*

In all the rural development programmes executed through DRDAS one witnessed lack of people's involvement. Even where P.R. institutions implement these programmes, they only function as agencies of the government to implement the programmes according to targets, procedures and programme contents laid down from above. There is very little local adaption. Little attention is paid to the local resource endowment and its utilisation for faster rural development. No effort is made to educate beneficiaries about the genesis of schemes and benefit likely to accrue to them. This results in leakage of funds and improper utilisation of assistance given.

The needs in this regard are thus two-folds:

(i) Greater involvement of representatives of local institutions at the village, block and district levels in planning and implementation of the rural development programme, and

(ii) Education of beneficiary groups for raising their consciousness and knowledge about the schemes and help they can seek from various agencies of government for their betterment.

2. *Danger of Target Oriented Approach*

Various programmes of rural development have become high target oriented. Since programme reviews are done at the apex level in the government and results are announced every month. There is a composition to achieve targets. It has become a number game. The quality of the programme implementation accordingly suffers. Sometime inflated figures of achievement are given to cover one's failures. Then, there is the problem created by high expectancy. Once high performance is achieved in particular areas by sacrificing else where, this becomes a reference for adjudging future achievements. This raises pressures on the system and forces it to achieve targets in numbers by book or by rook. Since all such pressures are finally felt at the district level or block level it impairs their general efficiency.

3. *Growing Burdens on Local Administration*

There is a bewildering variety of development schemes under implementation at the district and block levels with their time bound implementation. Despite funds allowed under some schemes for provision of staff, etc. requisite strengthening has not taken place at the operating levels. This has affected the quality of supervision and planning. There is need for a detailed analysis of the work pressures at the block and district levels and for providing requisite staff for strengthening of the set up. This should be financed on 100 per cent basis by the Central Government.

4. *Others*

(i) Lack of aftercare

(ii) Lack of infrastructure

(iii) Problem of identification, and

(iv) Inadequate marketing facilities have also vitiated the progress.

With a view to solving these problems a few suggestions are mentioned here :

1. Need for integrated approach.
2. Greater emphasis on group activity.
3. Proper marketing arrangements for products of benefit units may be made.
4. To extend more benefit in remote areas.
5. Identification of beneficiaries should be done strictly as per government guidelines.
6. Adequate veterinary facilities should be provided in every village.
7. Limit of poverty line may be raised.
8. Banks may be asked to revise their repayment schedules, and
9. Provision of legal aid for beneficiaries.

Rural Development on Growth Centre Basis

Spatial distribution of human settlements take place on the basis of hierarchy of service facilities provided by various growth centres to their hinterland. During the hey days of community development and Panchayati Raj. there was considerable emphasis on the training. With the declining interest in Panchayati Raj in the country, the training of personnel got neglected. Fortunately, the ministry of rural development decided to assist states in building up training facilities for rural development. However, the implementation of the scheme has been very tardy so far. The problem areas in this regard are :

(i) Centralisation of sanctioning powers at the level of ministry of rural development.

(ii) Release of assistance has been made dependent on the recommendations of an expert group which has members from different places. This group is unable to meet regularly with the result that processing of proposals get delayed.

(iii) Lack of realisation about the contribution which

training can make for better implementation of programme.

(iv) Inability of the State Government to provide their matching share under the scheme.

The following measures need to be taken for mounting adequate training efforts for better implementation of programmes during the Seventh Five Year Plan :

(i) Streamlining of the present procedure of rendering assistance of states by the Centre for training in rural development.

(ii) Creation of mutually beneficial collaborative arrangements for training and research between NIRD and Apex State Training Institutions.

(iii) Preparation of a perspective plan for development for every state training institutions.

(iv) Preparation of training material.

(v) Assessment of training needs for various functionaries and development of appropriate syllabus and organisation of adequate number of courses to meet these training needs, and

(vi) Research and evaluation studies.

The quality of personnel would be a crucial determinant of the successful implementation of various rural development programmes. Besides the training input, employment of appropriate personnel policies for placement of key functionaries at the district and block level would be essential.

To conclude, it may be suggested that the rural economy of Sikar may be further strengthened by formulating plans for the improvement of (i) environment and (ii) management at district, block and gram panchayat levels. In view of the emphasis on block level planning in the Seventh Five Year Plan, the role of the lead banks in preparing a corresponding block level credit plan has assumed great importance to lend appropriate support to the programmes for rural development.

Bibliography

Books

Andrae Brend. *The Economic of Tropical Agriculture Slough.* Common Wealth Agriculture Bureau, 1980.

Arnon Issac. *Modernisation of Agriculture in Developing Countries.* John willy & Sons, 1981.

Arora, R.C. *Development of Agriculture and Allied Sectors.* S. Chand & Co. Pvt. Ltd., New Delhi, 1976.

Arora, R.C, *Integrated Rural Development.* S. Chand & Co. Pvt. Ltd., New Delhi, 1979.

Agarwal, A.R. *Indian Economy.* 6th ed. Vikas, New Delhi, 1981.

Agarwal, A.N. *Indian Agriculture, Problem Progress and Perspects.* Vikas, New Delhi, 1980.

Anne, B. *et al., Labour Absorption in Agriculture, Theoretical Analysis and Empirical Investigations.* Oxford University Press, 1985.

Bapna, S.L. *Economic & Social Publications of Green Revolution A Case Study of Kota District.* AERC Delhi, 1970.

Basu, S.K. *Commercial Bank and Agricultural Credit, A Study in Regional Disparity in India.* Allied Publications, New Delhi, 1979.

Bergamann Theodor. *Mechanization of Indian Farming, Obstacles and Prospects.* Population Parkashan, Bombay, 1978.

Behari, M. and B. Behari. *Indian Economy Since Independence.* D.K., Delhi, 1983.

Bhargava, B.S. *Minor Irrigation Development in India, A Review.* Ashish Publishing House, New Delhi, 1980.

Bhattacharya, V. *New Faces of Rural India : March of Twenty Point Programme.* Metropolitan, New Delhi, 1982.

Bhattacharya, S.N. *Rural Development in India and Other Developing Countries,* Metropolitan, New Delhi, 1983.

Chatterji, A. *A Study of Agriculture Growth.* Indian Journal of Agricultural Economics, Vol. XXI, No 4, October-December, pp. 192-200, 1966.

Chennul, V.V. and K.M. Mehrotra. *Plant Protection in India. Retrospective and Prospects.* Commerce Annual Number, 1979.

Choubey, B.N. *Institutional Finance for Agricultural Development.* Shubhada Saraswat, Pune, 1977.

Chowdhry, D. Paul. *New Partnership in Rural Development.* M.N. Publications. New Delhi, 1978.

Dagli, Vadilal. *Infrastructure for Indian Economy.* Vora, Bombay 1970.

Dantawala, M.L. *Agricultural Policy in India since Independence.* Orient Longman, Bombay, 1979.

Dasgupta, B. *The New Agrarian Technology and India.* Macmillan Press, India, 1980.

Dewan, M.L. *Agriculture and Rural Development in India, Case Study on the Dignity of Labour.* Concept, New Delhi, 1982.

Dhawan, B.D. *Development of Tubewell Irrigation in India.* New Delhi, 1982.

Dhanagre, D.N. *Rural Transformation in India, Challenges & Prospects.* J.S.S. Institute of Economic Research, Dharwad, 1982.

Enayat, A. *et al. Regional Planning with Reference to India.* Oriental, New Delhi, 1980.

Enyedi, G. *et al. The Effect of Modern Agriculture on Rural Development.* Pergman Press, 1982.

Ezekial, H. *The Economic Times Statistical Survey of the Indian Economy.* Vikas, New Delhi, 1984.

Fakhrul Hasan. *Introduction to Welfare Economics.* Area, Bombay, 1963.

George, P.T. *Ceilings on Land Holdings in India.* Review National Institute of Rural Development, Hyderabad, 1979.

Gill, M. Singh. *Agriculture Cooperatives.* Vikas, New Delhi, 1983.

Gruffin, K. *The Political Economy of Agrarian Change.* The Macmillan Press Ltd., Delhi. 1974.

Hanumanth Rao, C.M. *Technological Changes and Distribution of Gains in Indian Agriculture.* Macmillan Press, Delhi 1975.

Hussain. *Agricultural Geography.* Inter India Publications,

New Delhi, 1979.

Kalhon, A.S. *A New Deal for Farmers, Ensuring Better Terms of Track. The Times of India*, July 1981.

Kalhon and Gurbachan Singh. *Social and Economic Implications of Large Scale Introduction of High Yielding Varieties of Wheat in the Punjab with Special Reference to Ferozpur District.* Punjab Agricultural University, Ludhiana.

Kamath, M.G. *A Dictionary of Indian Agriculture.* Allied Publishers, 1972.

Khan, A.H. *Ten Decades of Rural Development.* Michigan State University, 1978.

Khusro, A.M. *Return to Scale in Indian Agriculture.* Indian Journal of Agricultural Economics. Oct.-Dec., Bombay, 1964.

Khurodoy, K.M. *Dairying in India, A Review.* Asia Publishing House, Bombay, 1975.

Kohlon, A.S. *et al. Agriculture Price Policy in India.* New Delhi 1483.

Lal, A.K. *Politics and Poverty—A Study of Bonded Labour.* Chetana Publications, New Delhi, 1977.

Laster, R.B. *The Twenty-ninth Day, Accounting. Human Needs and Number to the Earth's Resources.* Radhakrishan Prakashan, New Delhi, 1979.

Laxminarayan, H. and Others. *Impact of Harvest Combines on Labour, Use Crop Pattern and Productivity, Rabi & Kharif.* Universty of Delhi, 1979.

Malasis, L. *Agriculture and Development Process.* The UNESCO Press, UNESCO, 1975.

Mandal, R.B. *Planned Development of Rural Settlement.* Concept, New Delhi, 1981.

Mishra, R.P. and K.V. Sundaram. *Multi-level Planning in Integrated Rural Development in India.* Heritage, New Delhi, 1980.

Mishra, S.N. and K. Sharma. *Problems and Prospects of Rural Development in India.* Uppal, New Delhi, 1983.

Nair Kusum. *Indian Agriculture after the Green Revolution.* University of Chicago Press, Chicago, 1979.

Narjundappa, D.M. *Area Planning and Rural Development.* Associates Publishing House, 1981.

Narula, R.K. and V. Gopalkrishna. *Agriculture and Rural*

Advances by Commercial Banks. UDH, New Delhi, 1984.

Nihal Chand. *Rural Economics.* UDH, New Delhi, 1984.

Oommen, T.K. *From Mobilization to Institutionalisation The Dynamics of Agrarian Movement in 20th Century.* Bombay, 1985.

Panchandikar, K.C. and J. Panchandikar. *Rural Modernisation in India. A Study in Developmental Structure.* Population, Bombay, 1978.

Patel, K.V. and S.M.Patel. *Economics of Rural Electrification and Lift Irrigation.* National Institute of Bank Management, Ahmedabad, 1969.

Patel, K.V. and A.C. Shah. and L.D. Mello. *Rural Economics.* Himalaya Publishing House, Bombay, 1984.

Prasad, N. and H.D. Gagneja. *Rural Economics.* B.R. Publishing Corporation, Delhi, 1984.

Rao, V.K.R.V. *Food Nutrition and Poverty in India.* Vikas Publishing House, New Delhi, 1982

Rao, K.Y.V. *Present Farming and Growth of Capitalism in Indian Agriculture.* Vishalandhra Publishing House, Vijayawada, 1985.

Rane, A.A. *Economics of Agriculture.* Atlantic, New Delhi, 1985.

Rao, R.V. *Rural Industrialisation in India.* Concept, New Delhi, 1978.

Rudder Dutt and K.P.M. Sunderum. *Indian Economy.* S.Chand & Co. Ltd., Delhi, 1982-83.

Saini, G.R. *Farm Size, Resources—Use Efficiency and Income Distribution*—A Study in Indian Agriculture with special reference to Uttar Pradesh and Punjab. Allied Publishers, New Delhi, 1979.

Sen Sunil. *Agrarian Relation in India.* People Publishing House, New Delhi, 1979.

Shah, C.H. and C.N. Vakil. *Agriculture Development of India and Problems.* Orient Longman, Bombay, 1979.

Singh, Inderjit. *The Small Farmers and the* Landless in South Asia. World Bank Staff Paper No. 320, World Bank, Washington, Feb. 1979.

Singhal, S.P. and P. Kelley. *Amul and Experiment in Rural Economic Development.* MacMillan, New Delhi, 1981.

Subramaniam, C. *The New Strategy in Indian Agriculture*

Vikas Publishing House, 1979.

Subramaniam, C. *The New Strategy in Indian Agriculture.* Vikas Publishing House, 1979.

Thingalaya, N.K. and B.S. Damodar. *Evaluation of the Implementation of District Credit Plan.* Economic Research and Planning Department, Syndicate Bank, 1980.

Thekkamalai, S.S. *Rural Development and Social Change in India.* D.K., New Delhi, 1983.

Tod James. *Annals and Antiquities of Rajasthan.*

Wadhawa, C.D. *Rural Bank for Rural Development.* An analysis of the working of Regional Banks in India with two case Studies. MacMillam, New Delhi, India, 1980.

Indian Society of Agricultural Economics, Delhi.

1. Land Tenure in India, 1946.
2. A socio-economic Survey of Bhuvet, 1949.
3. Introduction to Rural Sociology in India, 1953.
4. Co-operatives in Kodinar, 1952.
5. Studies in Indian Agricultural Economics, 1958.
6. Problems of Small Farmers Report on an enquiry into the problems of low-income farmers in Kodinar Taluka, 1958.
7. Post-war Agricultural Problems and Policies in India, 1951.

Indian Agriculture Research Institute. Scientific basis of Indian Agriculture, Seventy-five years of Service, New Delhi. The Author, 1980.

Indian Council of Agricultural Research, Agriculture Research in India. Achievements and Outlook, New Delhi. The Author, 1972.

Indian Council of Social Science & Research. Alternatives in Agricultural Development, An ICSSR Working Group Report. New Delhi Allied, 1980.

National Council of Applied Economic Research. Implication of Tractorisation for Farm Employment. Productivity and Income, 2 vols., New Delhi, 1980.

National Institute of Rural Development. Rural Development in India. Some Facts, Hyderabad, 1981.

Venkatappiah, B. and V.K.R.V. Rao. *Cooperation*—Two Perspectives Indian Society for Studies in Cooperation, Pune, 1982.

Reports

1. Report of the Royal Commission on Agriculture in India, 1926.
2. Report of the Royal Commission on Labour, 1981.
3. Report of the Central Banking Enquiry Committee, 1981.
4. Report of the Cooperation in India (Maclegan Committee, 1949).
5. Report of the Agricultural Finance Sub-Committee (Gadgil Committee, 1949).
6. Report of the Agrarian Reform Committee (Kumarappa Committee, 1950).
7. Report of the Rural Banking Enquiry Committee, 1981.
8. Report of the Division Forest Officer, Jaipur, 1981.
9. Report of the District Medical and Health Officer, 1984.
10. Report of the Inspector of Schools, Sikar, 1984.
11. Report of Agricultural Labour Inquiry Committee. 1981.
12. Report of the State Agricultural Marketing Officer, Rajasthan, 1984.
13. Report of Chief Engineer, P.W.D., Rajasthan, 1984.
14. Report of the Assistant Registrar, Cooperative Societies, Sikar, 1983-84.
15. Report of the Registrar, Cooperative Societies, Rajasthan 1984.
16. Report of the Director, Consolidation of Holdings, Rajasthan, 1984.
17. Report of the Deputy Collector, Sikar, 1984.
18. Report of the Secretary, Rajasthan Khadi & Village Industries Board, 1983.
19. Annual Reports of the State Agricultural Engineer, Rajasthan, 1981, 82, 83 and 1984.
20. Report of the Food Grains Enquiry Committee, 1957.
21. Report of Minor Irrigation Committee, 1957.
22. Report of the Working Group on Additional Storage Facilities in Rural Areas and Related Matters, 1979.
23. Report of the Foodgrain Enquiry Committee, 1957.
24. District Census Handbook, Sikar, 1981.

25. Statistics Abstract, Rajasthan, 1981.
26. Ministry of Labour—

(i) Rural Labour Enquiry 1974-75
(ii) Annual Report, 1979-80

27. Ministry of Finance—

(i) Report of the Seventh Finance Commission, 1978.
(ii) Government of India, Economic Survey, 1982, 83 and 84.

28. Planning Commission--

(i) First Five Year Plan, 1951-55
(ii) Draft Seventh Plan
(iii) Report of the Working Group on Block Level Planning (Dantawala Working Group) 1978.
(iv) Evaluation Study of Rural Industries Project, 1978.
(v) Report on Evaluation Study of Small Farmers, Marginal Farmers and Agricultural Labourers, 1979.

29. Ministry of Rural Reconstruction, Manual on Integrated Rural Development, 1981.
30. Reserve Bank of India :

(i) Rural Credit Review Committee, 1966.
(ii) Review Committee Report for Instituting Credit for Agriculture and Rural Development, 1979.
(iii) Lead Bank Scheme, District Credit Plan, New Guidelines, Role of the Reserve Bank of India in the sphere of Rural Credit, RBI, 1980.
(iv) Report on Trade and Progress of Banking in India, 1980-81
(v) Guidelines to Institutional Structure and Rural Development Institution in India, Organisation of Government Machinery and their Functions, College of Agricultural Banking, RBI, 1981.

31. Report of the Committee to Review Arrangements for Institutional Credit for Agriculture and Rural Development, Bombay, 1981.
32. Working Group on Role of Banks in Implementation of the New 20-Point Programme (Ghosh Working Group), June, 1982.
33. Report of the Rural Creative Survey Committee, 1951.
34. Technical Report of all India Rural Credit Survey, 1951.
35. All India Rural Credit Survey, General Report.
36. Report of the Agricultural Finance, Sub-Committee, 1945.

Periodicals

(Yearly)

1. *Asia Year Book*, Hong Kong

(Bi-annual)

2. *Economic Administration Review*, Department of EAFM, University of Rajasthan, Jaipur.
3. *American Journal of Economics and Sociology*, USA.
4. *Artha Vikar*, Dept. of Economics, Sardar Patel University Vallabh Vidyanagar, Gujarat.
5. *Regional Studies*, USA.

(Quarterly)

6. *India Co-operative Review*, New Delhi.
7. *Indian Journal of Agricultural Economics*, Bombay.
8. *Indian Journal of Commerce*, Patna.
9. *Indian Economic Journal*, Bombay.
10. *Productivity*, New Delhi.
11. *Economy and Society*, London (England).
12. *Foreign Agriculture*, Washington DC, USA.
13. *Artha Vijocnana*, Poona.
14. *Economics*, England.
15. *Man Power*, New Delhi.
16. *Indian Economic Diary*, New Delhi.
17. *Land Economics*, USA.

(Monthly)

18. *Rural India*, Bombay.
19. *Economic Affairs*, Calcutta.
20. *Kurukshetra*, New Delhi.
21. *Reserve Bank of India Bulletin*, Bombay.

22. *Agriculture Situation in India*, Delhi.
23. *Monthly Commentry of Indian Economic Conditions*, New Delhi.
(Fortnightly)
24. *India Today*, New Delhi.
25. *Yojna*, New Delhi.
26. *Industrial Times*, Bombay.
27. *Economic Trends*, New Delhi.
28. *Southern Economist*, Bangalore.
29. *Co-operator*, New Delhi.
(Weekly)
30. *Eastern Economist*, New Delhi.
31. *Commerce*, Bombay.
32. *The Illustrated Weekly of India*, Bombay.
33. *Economic and Political Weekly*, Bombay.
(Dailies)
34. *The Economic Times*, New Delhi.
35. *The Financial Express*, Bombay.
36. *The Hindustan Times*, New Delhi.
37. *The Times of India*, New Delhi.
38. *The Rajasthan Patrika*, Jaipur.

Index